WORD 2021 FOR SENIORS

AN INSANELY SIMPLE GUIDE TO WORD PROCESSING

SCOTT LA COUNTE

ANAHEIM, CALIFORNIA
www.RidiculouslySimpleBooks.com

Copyright © 2021 by Scott La Counte.

All rights reserved. No part of this publication may be reproduced, distributed or transmitted in any form or by any means, including photocopying, recording, or other electronic or mechanical methods, without the prior written permission of the publisher, except in the case of brief quotations embodied in critical reviews and certain other noncommercial uses permitted by copyright law.

Limited Liability / Disclaimer of Warranty. While best efforts have been used in preparing this book, the author and publishers make no representations or warranties of any kind and assume no liabilities of any kind with respect to accuracy or completeness of the content and specifically the author nor publisher shall be held liable or responsible to any person or entity with respect to any loss or incidental or consequential damages caused or alleged to have been caused, directly, or indirectly without limitations, by the information or programs contained herein. Furthermore, readers should be aware that the Internet sites listed in this work may have changed or disappeared. This work is sold with the understanding that the advice inside may not be suitable in every situation.

Trademarks. Where trademarks are used in this book this infers no endorsement or any affiliation with this book. Any trademarks (including, but not limiting to, screenshots) used in this book are solely used for editorial and educational purposes.

Table of Contents

Introduction 6
The Word Crash Course 7
    Main Menus 8
    Collaborating on a Document 12
The Home Ribbon 15
Insert Ribbon 25
Draw Ribbon 46
Design Ribbon 49
Layout Ribbon 56
The Reference Ribbon 67
Mailings Ribbon 82
Review Ribbon 87
View Ribbon 94
Formatting Photos and Shapes 98
Let's Get Creative! 103
Accessibility 125
    Dictation and Read Aloud 125
    Zooming 130
Index 132

About the Author 134

Disclaimer: Please note, while every effort has been made to ensure accuracy, this book is not endorsed by the Microsoft Corporation and should be considered unofficial.

Introduction

There's a good chance you grew up with a typewriter. Typewriters weren't exactly feature creep. They could bold, italicize, and underline things, but that's about as deep as their functionality went.

Modern word processing does so much more! It checks your grammar, let's you coedit documents with others, even add pictures and multimedia. And when it comes to Word processing, there's one software that seems to rule over all: Microsoft Word.

This guide, which is based off of Word for Mac, will walk you over the features you need to know and how to use them. Don't worry if you have a PC—they work almost the same.

So if you're ready to get started, then let's create some beautiful documents together.

Note: this book is based off of *The Insanely Easy Guide to Word 2021*, but has an extra chapter on accessibility.

[1]
The Word Crash Course

If you are returning to Word after a break, then things might look a bit different. Microsoft is all about the ribbon now! Back in the day when we had to walk barefoot five miles in the snow, we had one menu! It never changed. That's good and bad.

It's bad if you hate change, but good if you like things to be more practical. The ribbon really is a game-changer. There are more options, but they also help you get things done more quickly.

Main Menus

While the ribbon is the main focal point of Word, there are a few other areas of note. First, if you are in full screen, move your mouse up north to the very top. That reveals a top menu bar as well as a mini toolbar in the blue area.

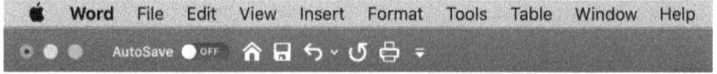

I'll cover the top menu later, but let's look really quick at that blue mini toolbar. To the far left is the close icon (red), minimize (greyed out in full screen), and enter / exit full screen (green); next to it is the AutoSave, which, if toggled to on, will save your work every few seconds; the next set you'll probably be familiar with—except for the house icon. The house icon will take you to the screen to open a new document or template. Next to it is save, undo, redo, and print.

Finally, there's a down arrow. If you want to add more mini shortcuts to this menu, you can click this; there are common commands that you can check off (or uncheck if you want them to disappear), or you can click More Commands to find more.

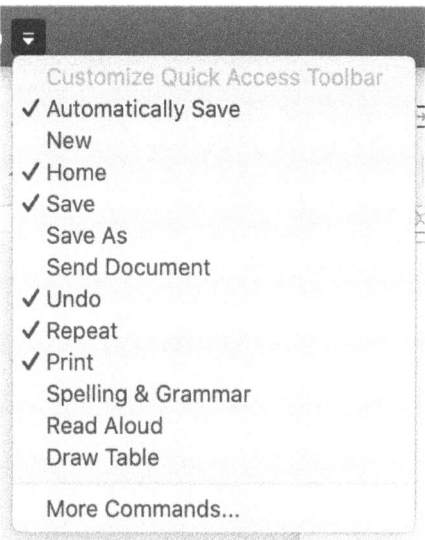

Over on the right size of the blue toolbar is a magnifying glass that you can use to find words in your document. The smile face icon is to leave feedback to Microsoft.

Down on the bottom of the screen, is a very thin toolbar that you probably won't use that much. To the bottom left, you can see the number of pages, words, and language. Those are all clickable.

Click the page numbers, and you'll get a thumbnail view of your pages.

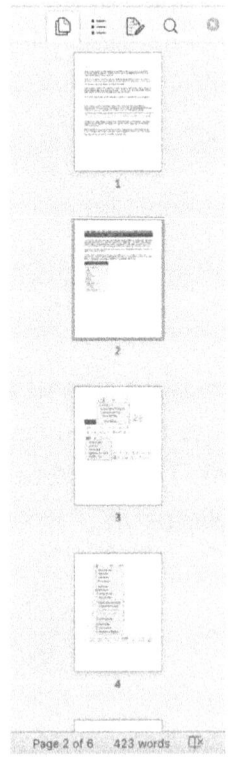

Click on the words and you'll get statistics about the text in your document.

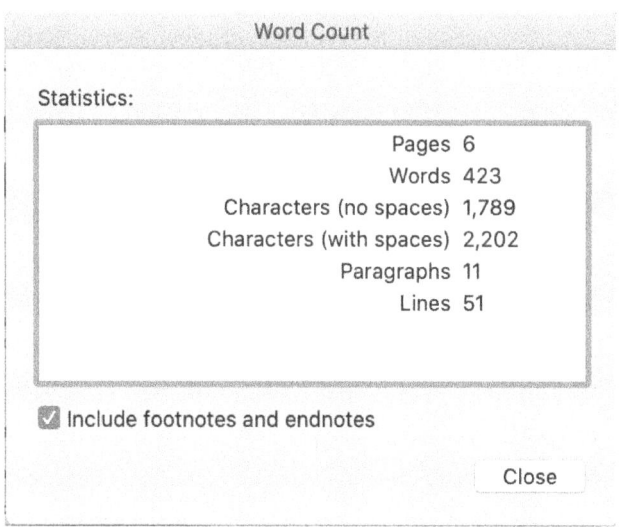

Finally, click on English and you can switch the language to another language.

Over in the bottom right is an area that lets you change your document view. So you can turn it into outline mode (which you probably won't use for most documents). The only area that you might find yourself using is the zoom; use the - / + on the bottom to zoom in or out.

Collaborating on a Document

Just above the main ribbons, you'll see two buttons: Share and Comments.

For many years, Word was a bit analog—if you wanted to share something, then you saved it, opened up your email client, attached it; Microsoft has been taking big strides to make this more streamline and more like what you would see in something like Google Docs. That's what this option is for.

Clicking on Share lets you name the file and then pick a place to save it—OneDrive in the example below, is a little like Microsoft's version of DropBox or Google Drive—it's cloud storage that's ideal for both sharing docs and storing them.

Share

Move or copy this document to the cloud to share:

Name: Micosoft Word

Place: OneDrive - Personal

Move   Upload

Send a Copy

You can still do it the old-fashioned way (i.e. email) by clicking on Send a Copy. That brings up a menu that lets you add it as an attachment to email.

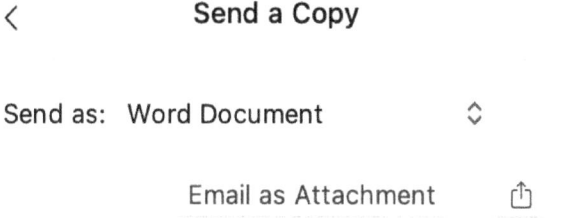

As you collaborate on a document, you can also go to the Review ribbon and turn the toggle on "Track Changes" from off to on. This will let the viewer see what changes you've made.

You can also highlight passages and click the comments option to add notes to the person—such as questions or suggestions.

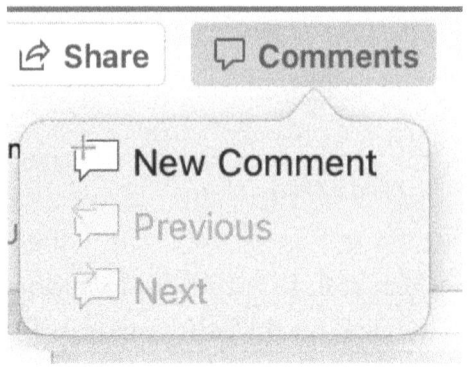

[2]
The Home Ribbon

I'm going to walk you through each of the menus one by one, starting with the one you'll use the most: the Home menu.

We'll go left to right, so starting with the first section, we have all of our copier icons. The big clipboard icon will let you do special kinds of copying—so if you want to copy text, for example, but don't want to copying the font size / font color, you could select to copy the text only.

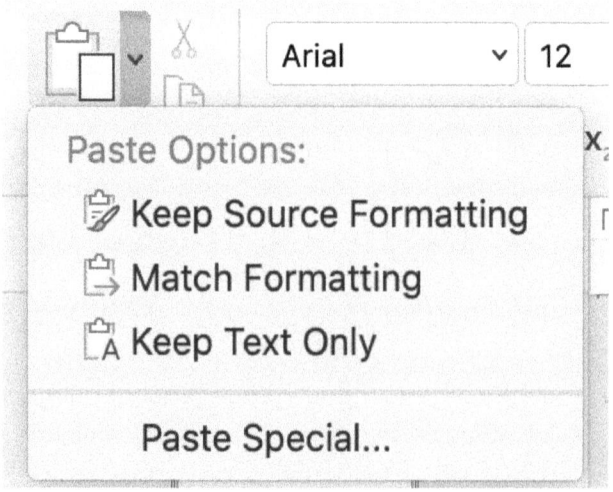

Next to that icon is the scissors and paste icon; this is the manual icon for copy / paste, but you can do this more quickly by remembering: Command+C for copy and Command+V for paste.

Below these icons is the format copier. With this icon you can copy the style / format of text. To use it, highlight the text you want to copy the style to, then highlight the text you want to apply the style to and click the icon again. This only copies the style—it doesn't copy the text. It's very useful if you want to copy things like font size and font color to different sections of a long document.

Next to this section is the formatting section. Most of these icons you've probably used before. Starting on the top row: font, font size, increase / decrease font size, paragraph case, and clear formatting.

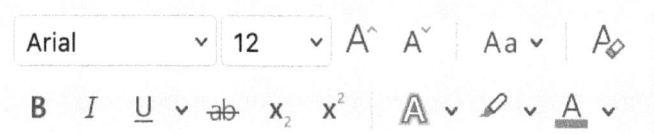

The Aa icon let's you change the words to all caps, sentence case, etc.

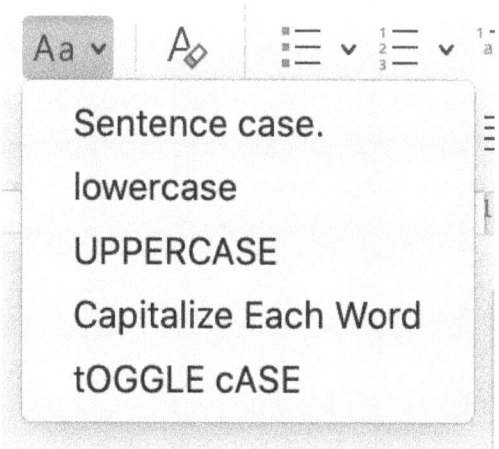

From left to right on the bottom row: bold, italics, underline (click the arrow next to that and you can make it a different underline style), strikethrough text, subscript, superscript, text effect (if you want the text, for example, to have a sort of glow), highlight color, and font color.

The next section is the layout of your text. Starting on the top row from left to right: create a bullet list (use the arrow to change the bullet formatting), number list (use the arrow to change number formatting), multiview list, indent over or indent back, sort, and the paragraph icon.

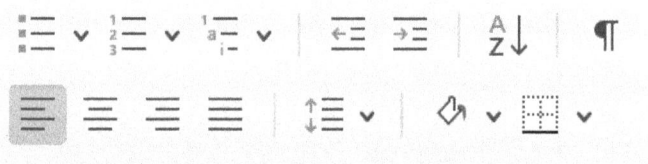

The paragraph icon will reveal where the space and paragraph breaks are; it can be useful if you're trying to make sure there's no extra spaces.

On the bottom row, from left to right: justification (left, center, right, and justify—meaning even), line and paragraph spacing, table fill, table borders. Click the arrow next to that and see all the border options (note: I'll cover tables a bit later, so don't stress too much about this section yet).

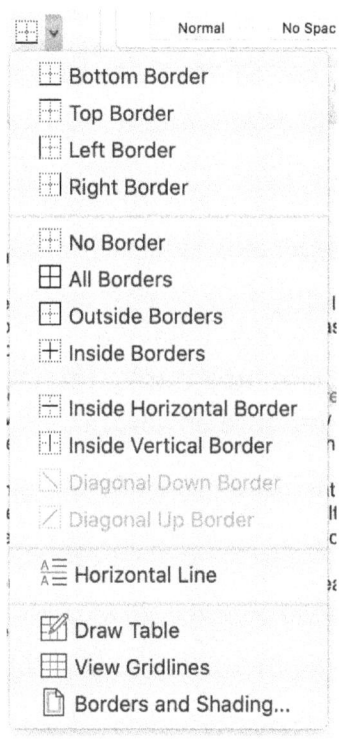

The next set of options is for styling your document. So if you have a heading, subheading, title, etc. What are the advantages of this?

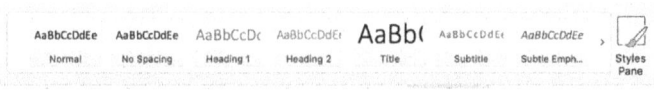

It's twofold:

It formats your text quickly; so you don't have to apply a certain font size to it each time you do a heading, for example.

It helps when you create your table of contents (if you are, in fact, creating one).

The below illustration shows a heading 1 and heading 2 in the navigation box (covered later in this book); so if you have a really long document (or you're writing a book), then using styles will help you navigate around.

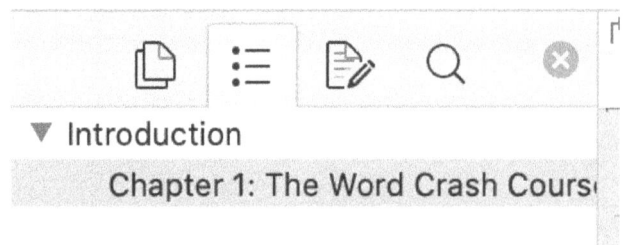

If you don't like the pre-defined style (for example, you want the heading 1 to be a different color or size), then highlight it; next, create the style you want in your document, then go to that style and right click it. From there, select "Update Heading 1 to Match Selection." Now whenever you use that style, it will use what you have just defined.

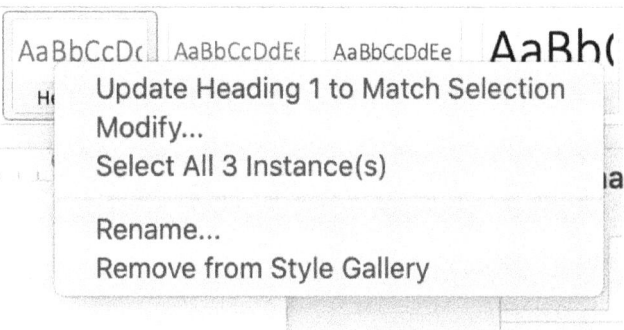

If you hover just a little below the style, there's an arrow; if you click it, it will reveal all the available styles.

The Styles Pane icon will also reveal all the styles, but it also gives you the option of creating a New Style.

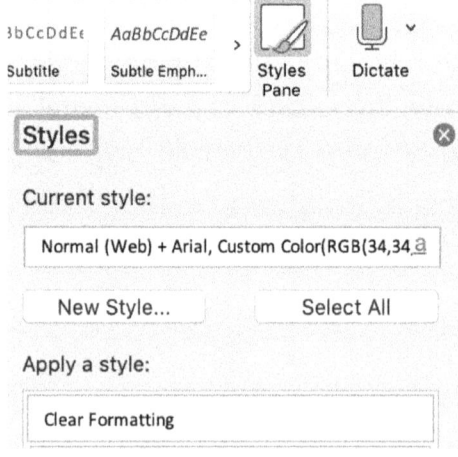

The last option under the Home ribbon is the Dictate icon; as the name suggests, this option allows you to do speak to text—it listens to what you say and transcribes it onto the page. The drop-down arrow lets you change the language that you are speaking—if you are speaking another language (or even speaking English with a UK or Canadian accent) make sure and update this so it transcribes correctly. To start it, just press the icon once.

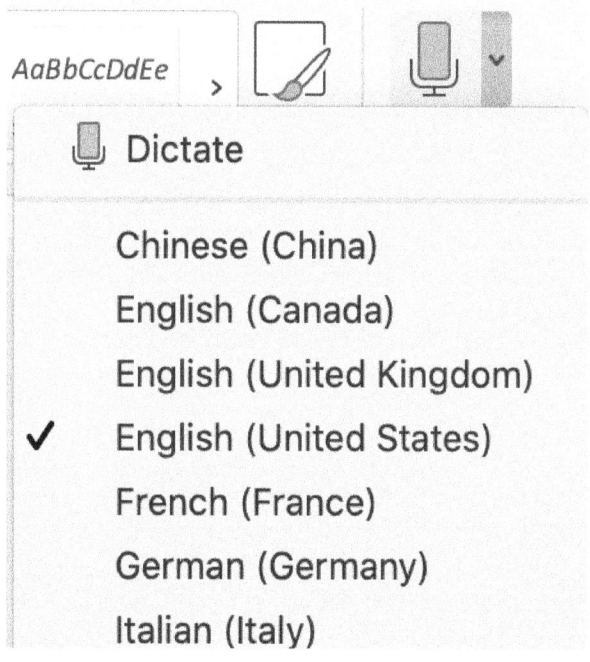

When you are recording a transcription, the dictation icon will change from the light blue to a white with a red record option. Click it again to turn it off.

[3]
Insert Ribbon

The days of inserting pictures are behind us; yes, you can still insert pictures in your Word doc, but Word does so much more than that now. You can insert media like movies and even Wikipedia if you turn the addon on.

Nearly anything that you want to add into Word can be done on the Insert ribbon.

The first thing you can insert—over on the far left—is Cover Page, Blank Page, or Page Break

(Page Break, which creates a new page in your document, can also be done by hitting Command+Return on your keyboard).

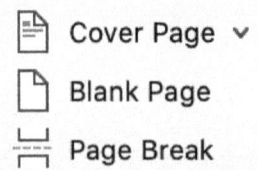

If you click the arrow next to Cover Page, you'll notice that there are a lot to choose from. To pick any, just click it one time with your mouse.

This creates a cover page in your document; from here, click (or double click) the text and type in text that you want to replace it with. Depending on who Word is registered to (when you set it up for the first time, someone else might have added their name—which is common if this is a family computer), you might see the wrong name.

The next icon is the Table insert. If you recall, there were options to format the Table in the

Home ribbon—you add it in this ribbon menu, but format it in the other.

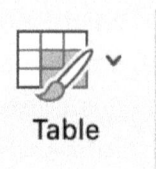
Table

When you click the down arrow on this icon, you'll be able to adjust how large or small you want the table to be by sliding your mouse over the boxes—note: you can make it bigger or smaller later if you pick the wrong size.

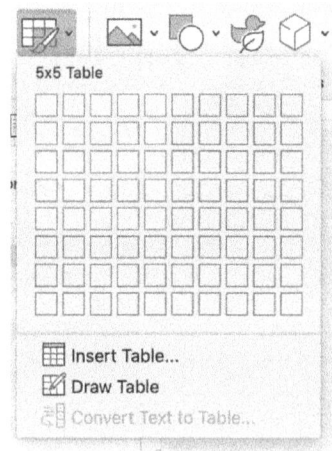

The most common thing you'll insert will probably be some kind of image or shape; you do so in the next group of icons.

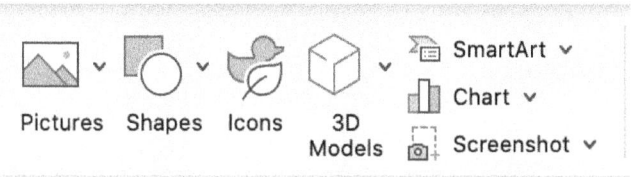

The first icon is pictures; when you click on it, you'll see that you can grab it from the photo browser (or gallery), a file, or an online source. Be careful here—using images online may be okay for school reports and family newsletters—if they're cited—but not okay to publish in a public place (i.e. the Internet).

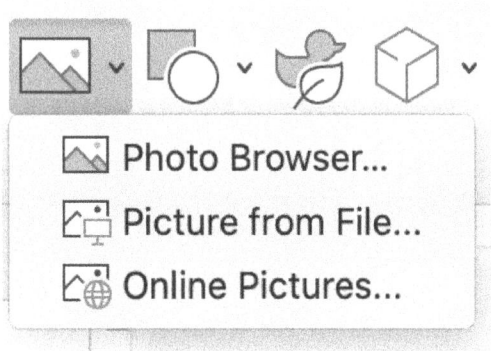

Next to photos is shapes. Shapes is a handy little tool that lets you put pre-defined shapes (such as circles and squares) into your document. Once you add a shape, you can adjust the size and color (I'll cover formatting images later in the book).

The next option is adding icons. Icons are basically common symbols for things. If you need the common symbol for handicap accessibility, for example. Like shapes, you are able to change the size and color. Just click the icons you want (you can pick multiple), then select the insert button at the bottom.

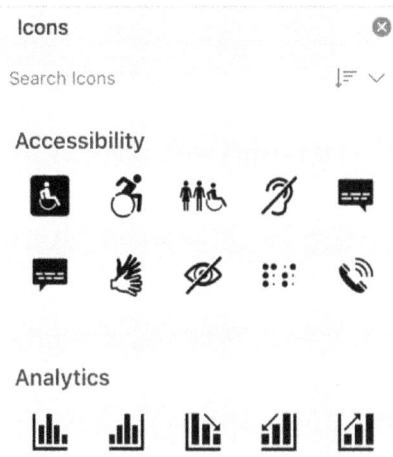

The last option is for 3D illustrations. Adding them is similar to photos and icons, but there's less you can do in terms of formatting. They're good for interactive reports, but not ideal for reports that you print out.

32 | *Word 2021 For Seniors*

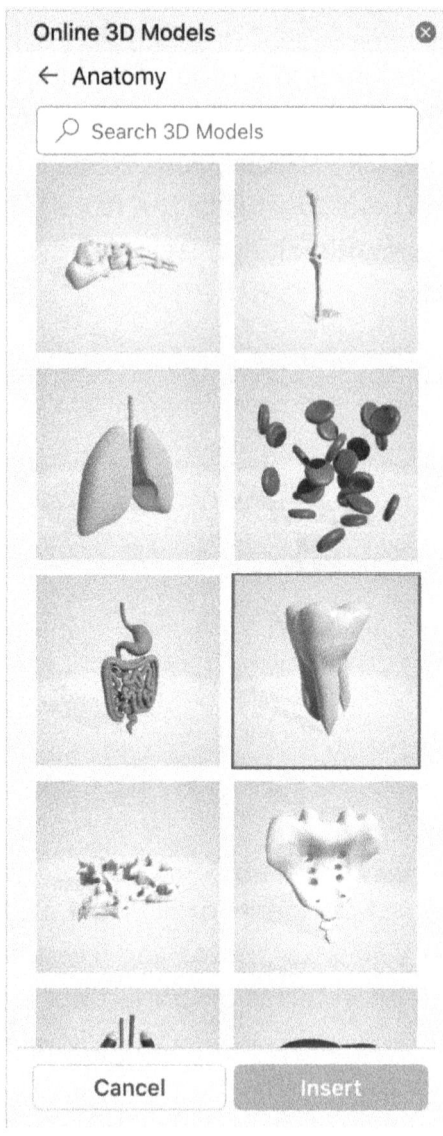

SmartArt is not art in the traditional sense. The way I see it is as a tool to help you create infographics. It's kind of like a combination of text and shapes. If you wanted to create a pyramid, for example, that shows the statistic, then you could do it with SmartArt.

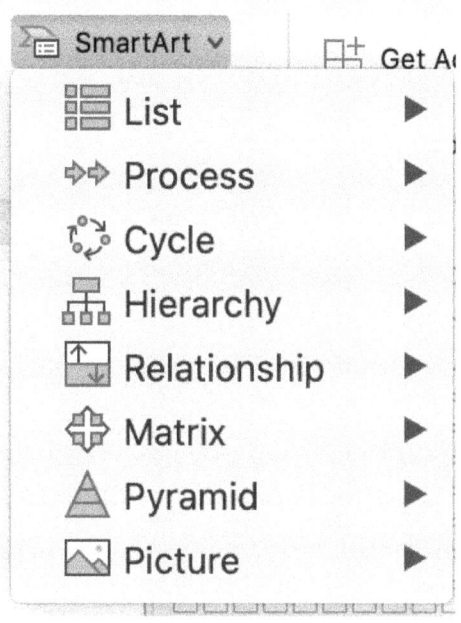

Charts are more commonly used in spreadsheets—and are easier to use if you have a spreadsheet because it can build a chart off the data you already have. Personally, I find it easier to create a chart in an Excel spreadsheet, and then copy and paste it into Word. If you want to build one in Word, then you would use this option.

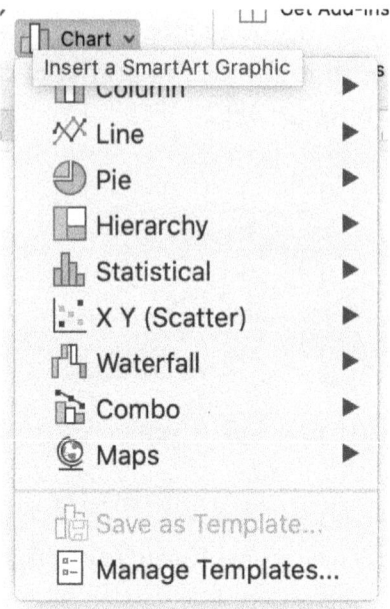

The last option in this section is to capture a screenshot. To use it, just click it once, then click the image preview that you see—or click Screen Clipping to crop it. You can also do screenshots natively on your Mac by pressing Command+Shift+3 (to screenshot the entire screen) or Command+Shift+4 (to screenshot a portion of the screen).

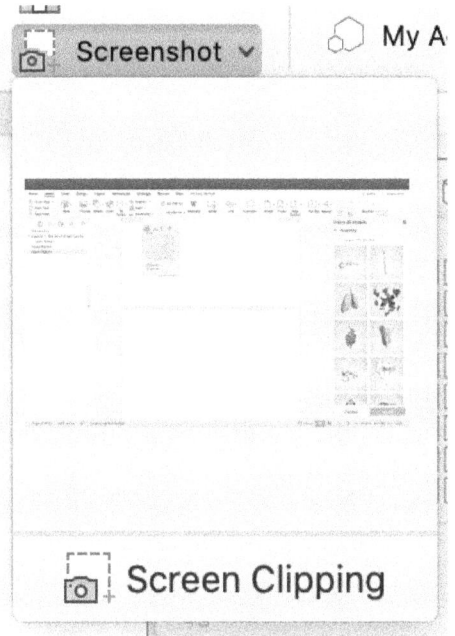

The next section is for adding addons; by default, you probably see a Wikipedia icon. There are hundreds of others, but you have to click "Get Add-ins" to add them. Addons help you be more productive without leaving the software—there are addons, for example, to help you translate or help with grammar.

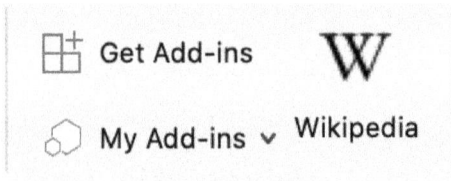

While most people will probably want to add an image or two at somepoint, movies and audio files might seem a little more unusual; afterall, you can't print movies or audio. Where this sort of media is useful is if you are create a document that will be used electronically.

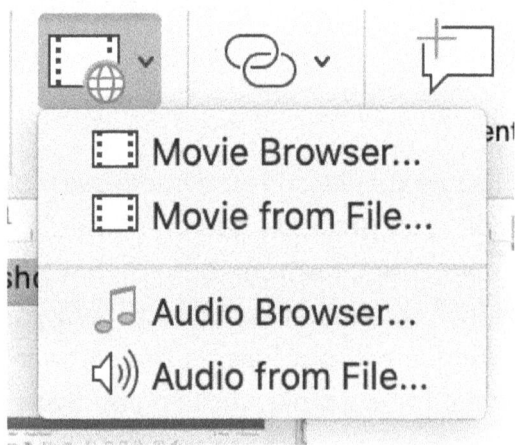

If you type a link in Word, it will automatically hyperlink it; if it doesn't, then you can use this section (or you can press Command+K). You can also use the Links icon to add bookmarks and crossreferences. When you add a bookmark, it does not appear different—it adds an invisible marker. But you can later add a reference to that section, and it essentially acts like a hyperlink to that section. It's especially useful in longer documents.

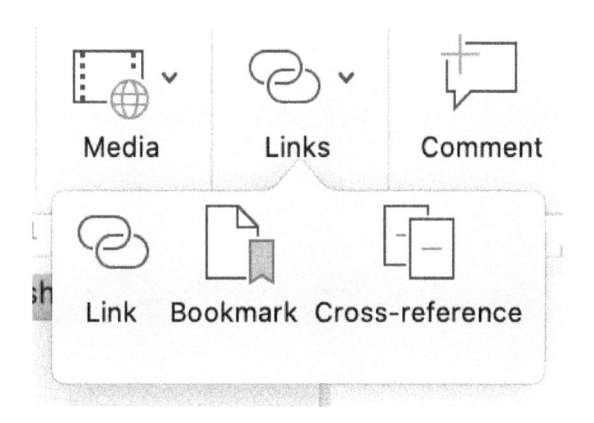

Comments are helpful when you are reviewing a document. You can highlight a word or sentence, then click comment, and leave a note to either yourself or the other person. If you email the document back to that person, they will see your note.

Insert Comment

The next section is for adding things to your document's header or footer (that section of your page on the top or bottom).

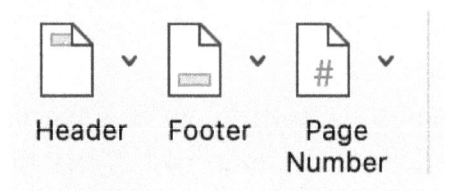

Header   Footer   Page Number

Clicking on the arrow lets you edit the format of the header or footer; do you want the page number on the right side, for example.

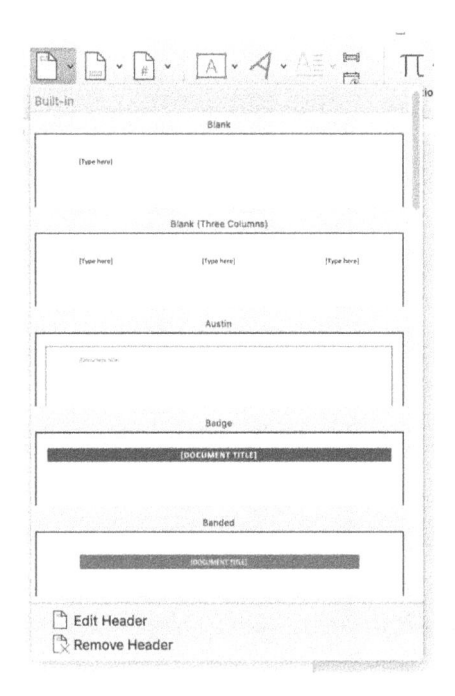

The page number will go in the header or footer area, but you can also click the arrow next to the page numbering to format how it will look and what number it will start with.

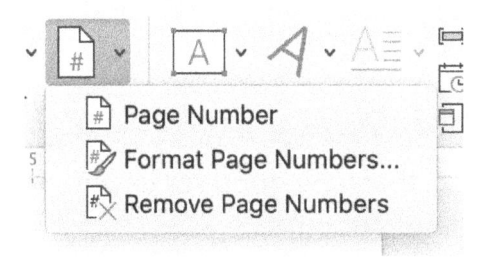

The next several options are all about applying different formats to your text.

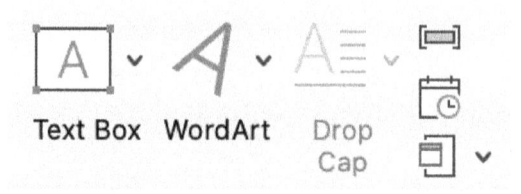

Text Box   WordArt   Drop Cap

For example, the first option lets you create a text box. A text box is exactly what it sounds like—a box with text inside of it. One reason it's useful is you can drag it around the page much as you would an image.

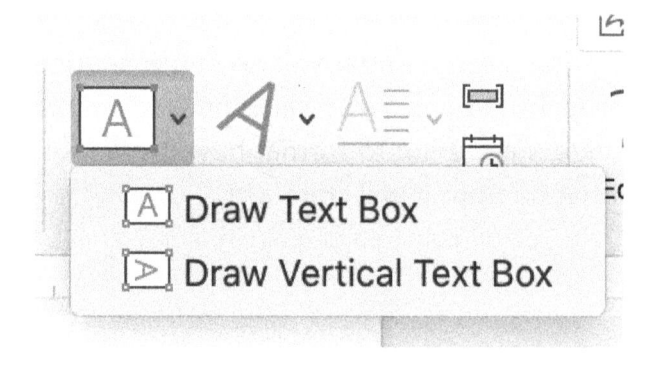

[A] Draw Text Box
[>] Draw Vertical Text Box

The next option, WordArt, turns your text into a graphic. It can be good for covers, as it helps your text stand out more.

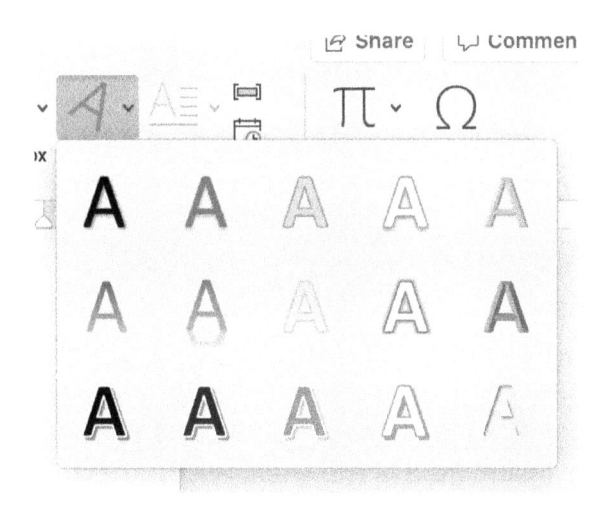

If you haven't highlighted any text, Drop Cap will be greyed out. Drop Cap is something you often do to the first paragraph of a longer document to help it stand out.

When you highlight the first paragraph (or any paragraph), you'll see all the formatting options for it.

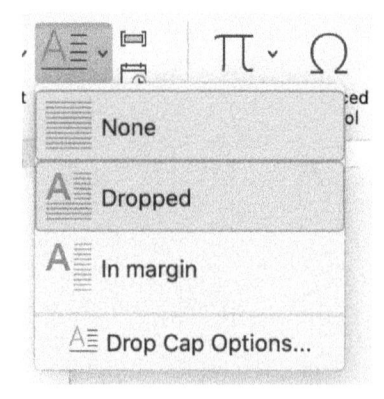

Insert field is the small button to the right of Drop Cap; it will become useful if you do labels, mailings and tables.

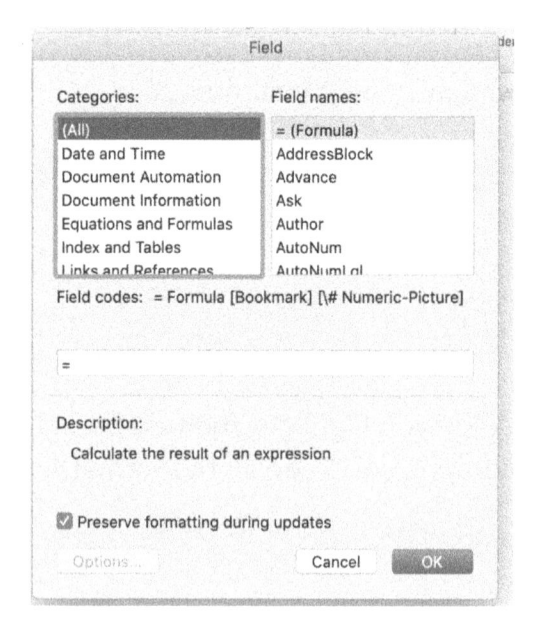

The icon below that changes how dates and times are inserted into your document. The benefit of using this option (vs. just manually typing it) is it can automatically update; so if the letter doesn't get done until the next day, the date will be updated.

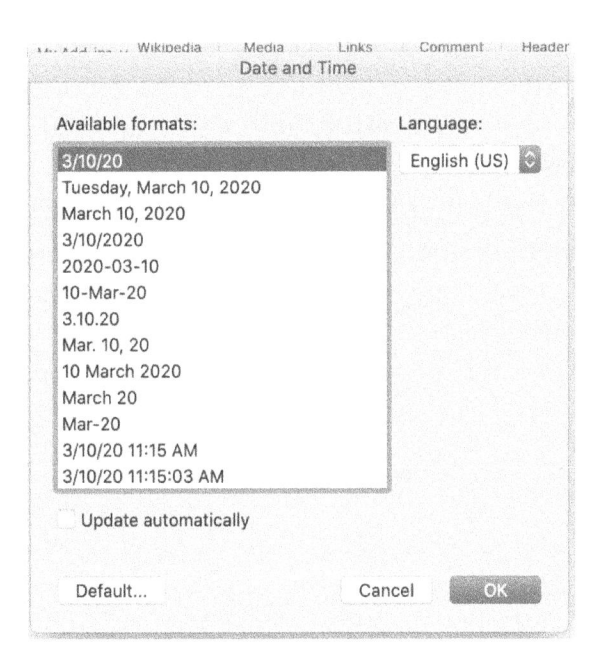

You can use the final option in this set of options to insert other files. If you are combining documents, you can either copy and paste them, or use this option. If the documents are particularly large, this takes less memory and can make the process much easier.

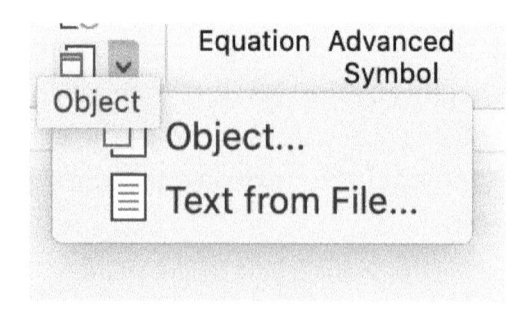

Unless you are a math student writing a dissertation, you probably won't have a lot of use for the last option; but if you ever need to add a complex math equation, this is where you would do it.

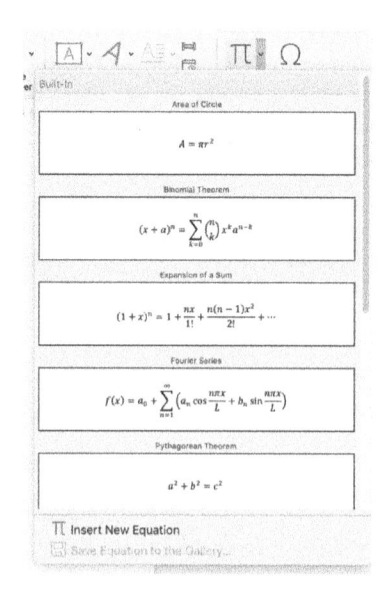

The final option is adding what Word calls "Advanced Symbols"; this is useful if you are typing something that has an odd character needed—a Greek symbol, for example, or an accent mark over a letter.

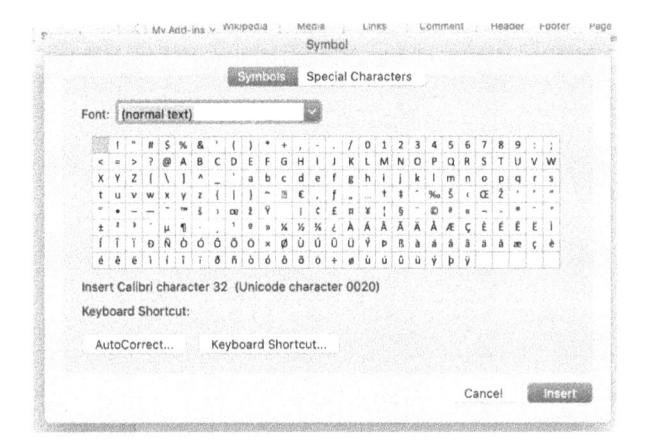

[4]

DRAW RIBBON

The draw ribbon is not exactly what it sounds like. Yes, you technically "draw" with it, but this isn't for sketching out your next masterpiece. The drawing here is more for marking up a document—drawing and highlighting passages, for example, to visually show where change is needed.

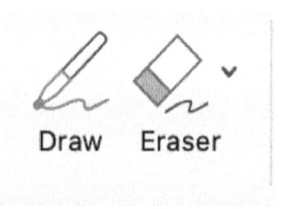

Draw   Eraser

To use the feature, click the pen that you want to use.

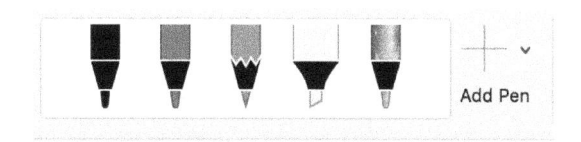

When you click the pen, you'll notice there's an arrow. Click that and you can adjust the color, brush / pen size, and, if available (not all pens have this) the effects.

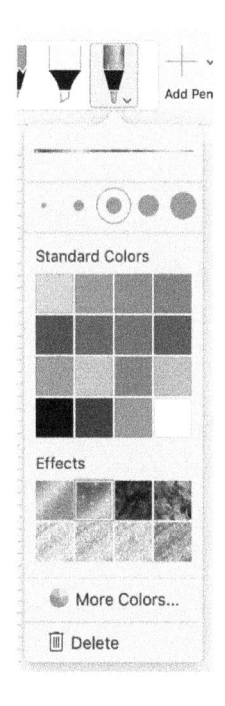

You can also use the plus button to add pens, and then make a custom color for it.

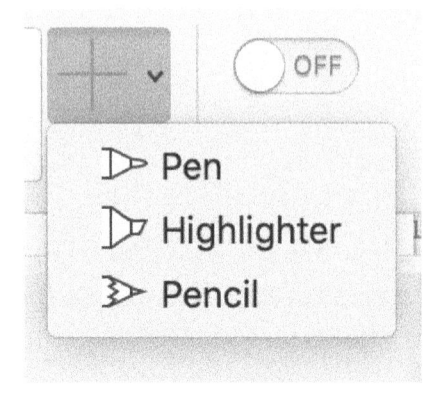

> Pen
> Highlighter
> Pencil

The last option is a toggle: Draw with Trackpad. This option lets you use your trackpad.

Draw with Trackpad

[5]
DESIGN RIBBON

The design ribbon is for changing the theme of your document; what does that mean? When you do a Heading 1 (or any style), what sizes and colors do you want it to be? Click on the Themes button and you'll see that there are dozens of themes to pick from.

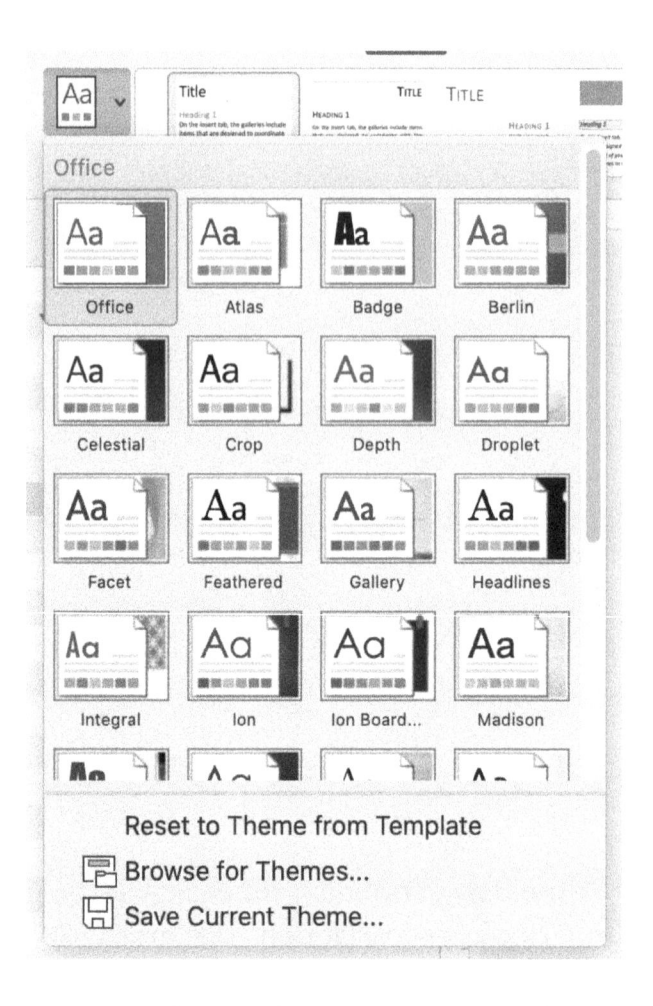

Once you pick your theme, you can apply a color scheme to the theme with the Colors icon.

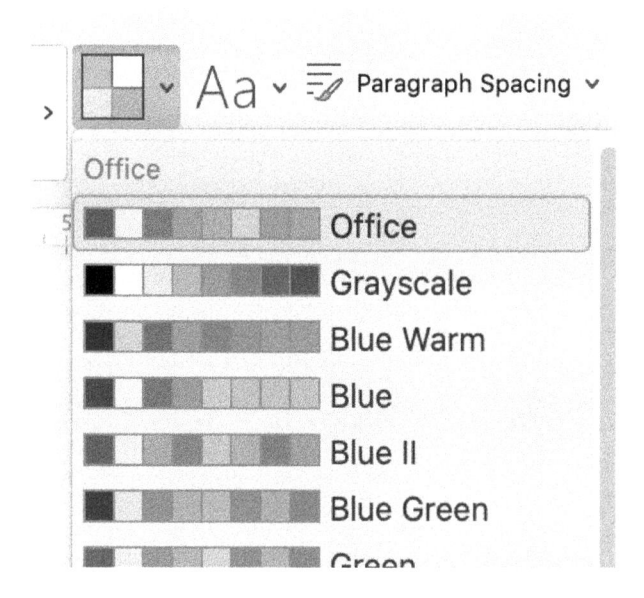

The Aa button lets you pick different fonts for your scheme.

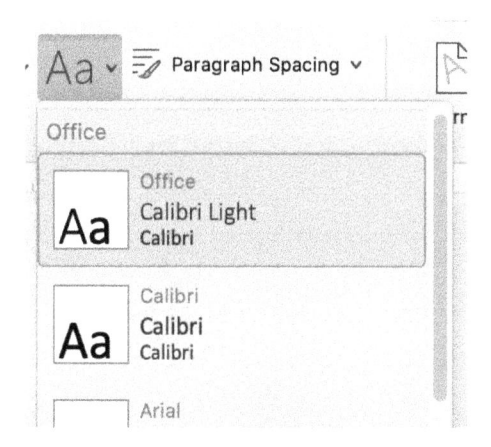

Finally, the Paragraph Spacing button lets you adjust the amount of spacing you see between lines.

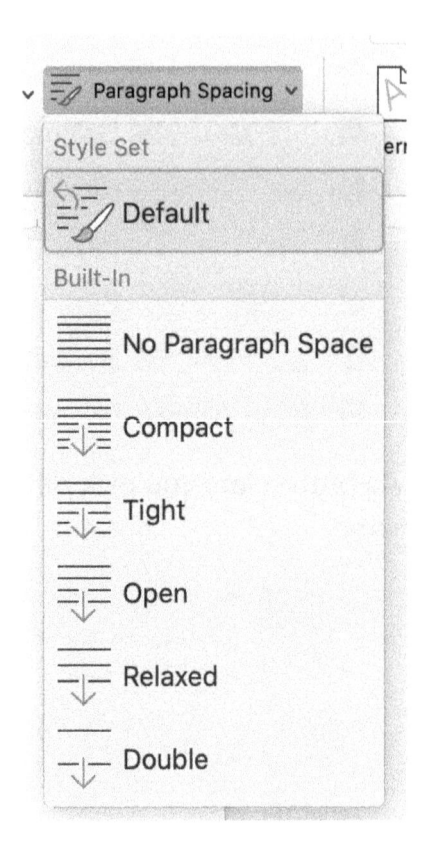

You can use the "Set as Default" to make this scheme the new default—that means anytime you open a new Word document, that's the scheme that will be applied.

⊘ Set as Default

On the far right are three more options.

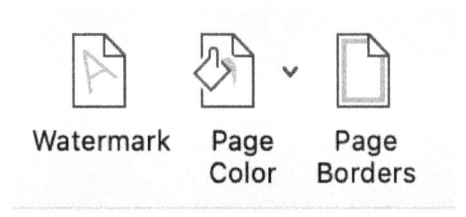

Watermark Page Color Page Borders

The first is a Watermark button. A watermark is an image that appears behind text—somewhat transparent. Typically it's used for something like a company logo. It may also be used to apply text—for example, you want it to say "Draft" as a watermark, so the person reading knows this is not the final copy.

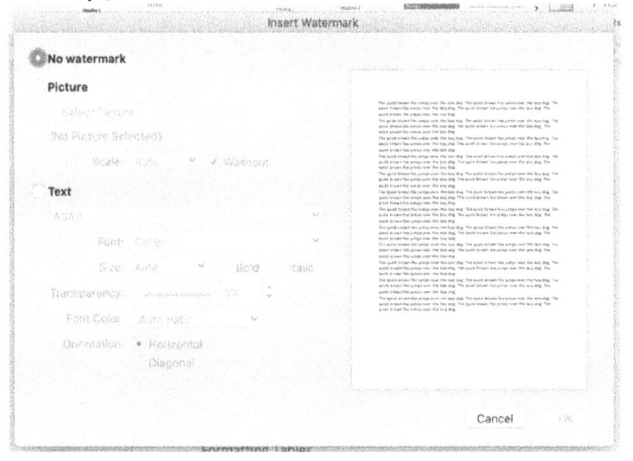

Next to the watermark button is the Page Color button. This will change the background color of your document; so the white background you see by default will be something different.

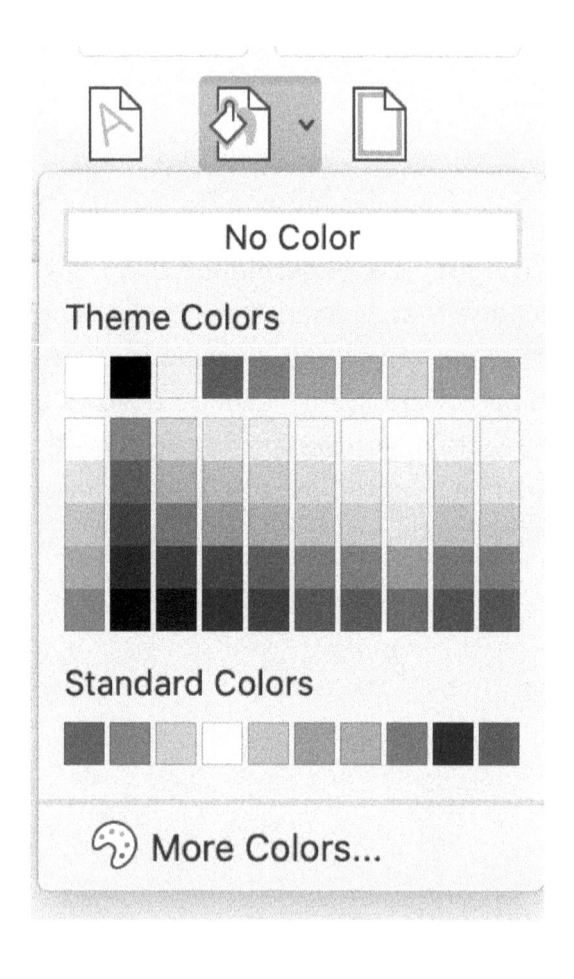

As the name implies, the last option is to apply a page border to your document.

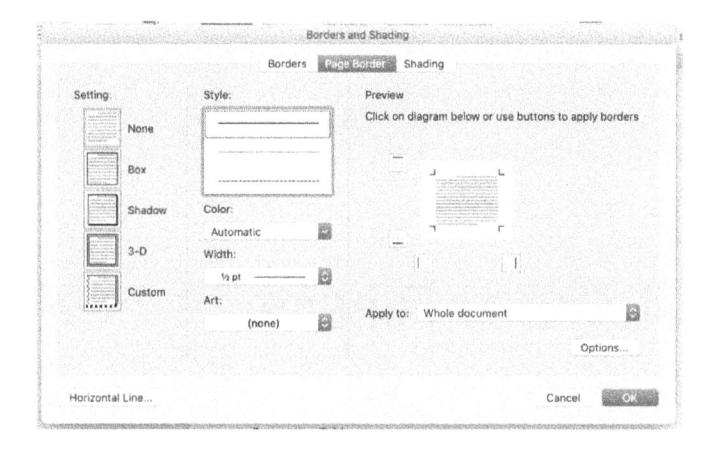

[6]
LAYOUT RIBBON

The Layout is where you'll be able to format how you want your document adjusted—do you want columns, what page margin, etc. You can also do "some" formatting to pictures here.

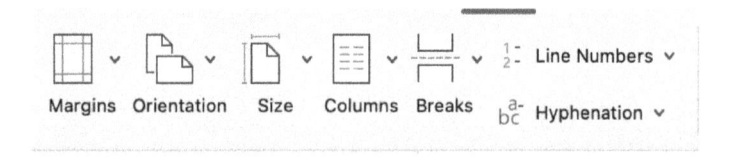

| Margins | Orientation | Size | Columns | Breaks | Line Numbers | Hyphenation |

The first option, for left to right, is the Margins button. If you click this, you'll have several predefined options, but can also create custom margins. So, for example, if you have to have 1.24 on all sides.

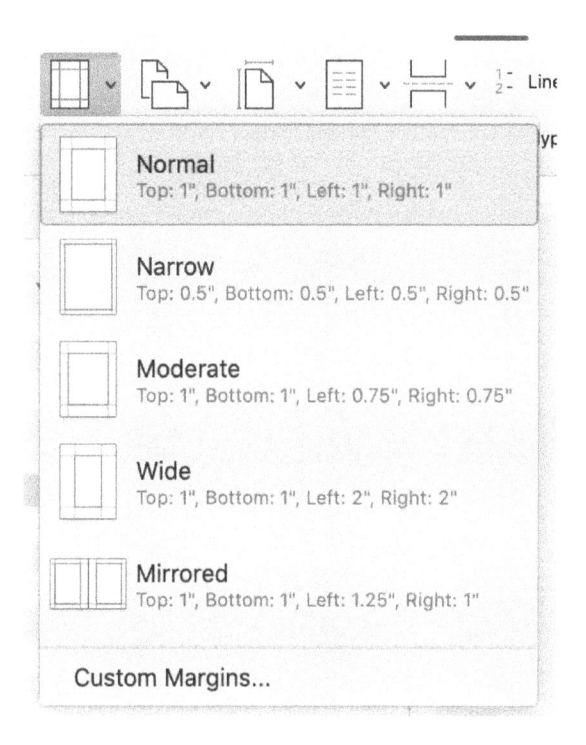

	Normal
	Top: 1", Bottom: 1", Left: 1", Right: 1"
	Narrow
	Top: 0.5", Bottom: 0.5", Left: 0.5", Right: 0.5"
	Moderate
	Top: 1", Bottom: 1", Left: 0.75", Right: 0.75"
	Wide
	Top: 1", Bottom: 1", Left: 2", Right: 2"
	Mirrored
	Top: 1", Bottom: 1", Left: 1.25", Right: 1"

Custom Margins...

The next option changes the orientation of the page. By default, it's portrait; you can use this button, however, to make the page turn horizontally to be landscape style (that means the page is now wide, but you won't be able to fit as many lines.

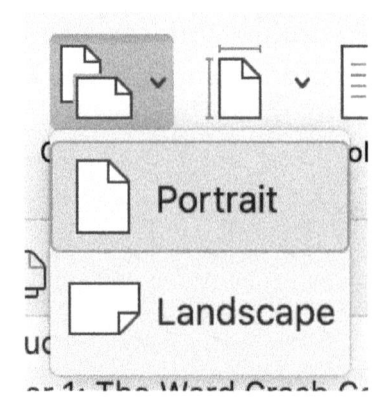

The next option lets you pick the paper size.

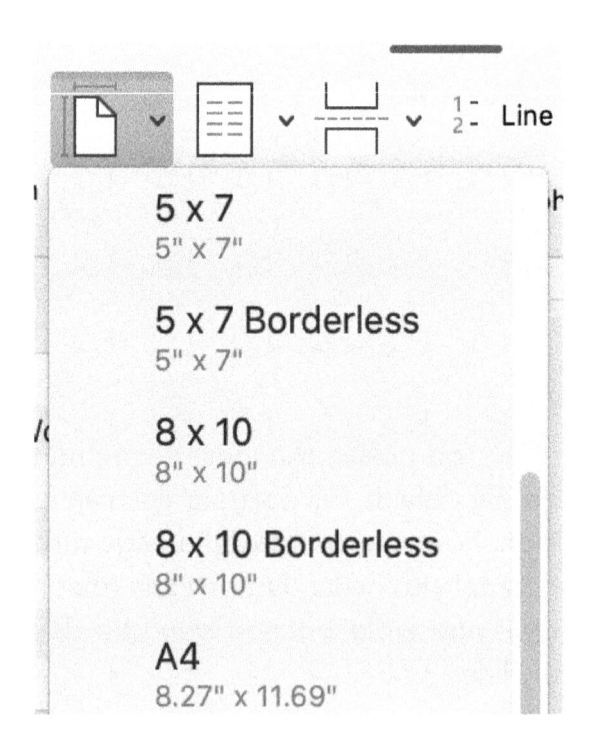

Paper size is all pre-defined. There's not option to create a custom size. So what do you do if the size you want isn't here? Go to File > Page Setup from the top menu. Then select Manage Custom Sizes. From here, you'll be able to create any size you want—but, depending on your printer, it may not print correctly.

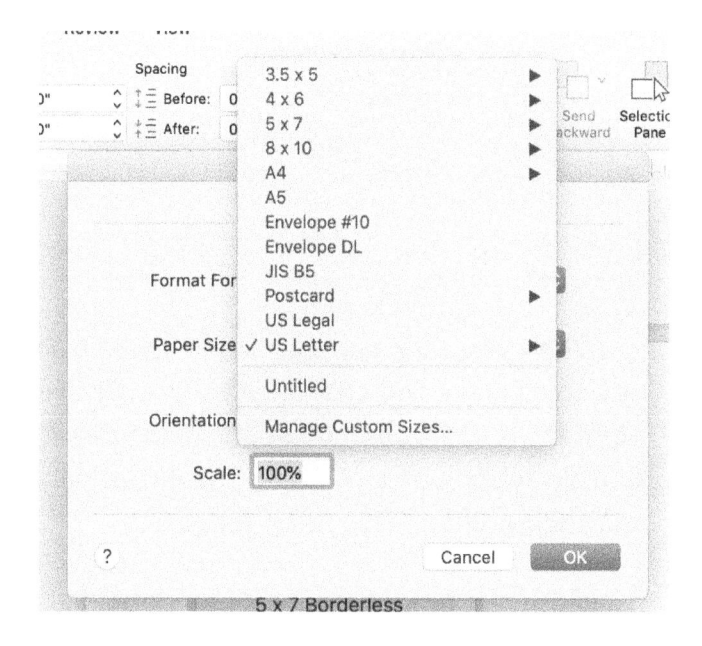

Columns is the next option; if you click that, you'll see several column options, but you can also click More Columns to see even more.

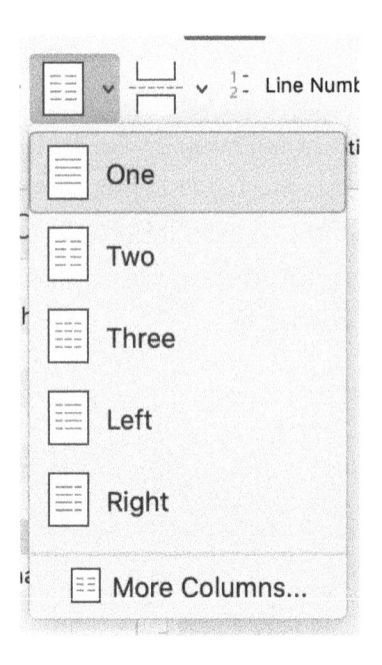

When you click more columns, there's also an option to make the column start at a different point in your document—so, for example, if you don't want columns to go on the entire page, you can change it to "This point forward."

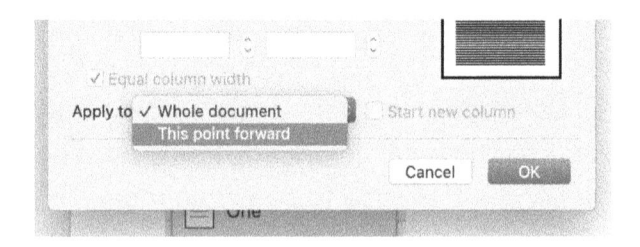

The easiest way to do a page break is to hit Command+Return on your keyboard, but you can also do it here as well; there's additionally an option to break columns—so if you haven't reached the bottom of a column yet, but you want to start on the next column over, then you can go here and create a break in the section.

The line numbering option isn't just to help you with double spacing; you can use it to decide if you want it for the whole document or just some of the sections.

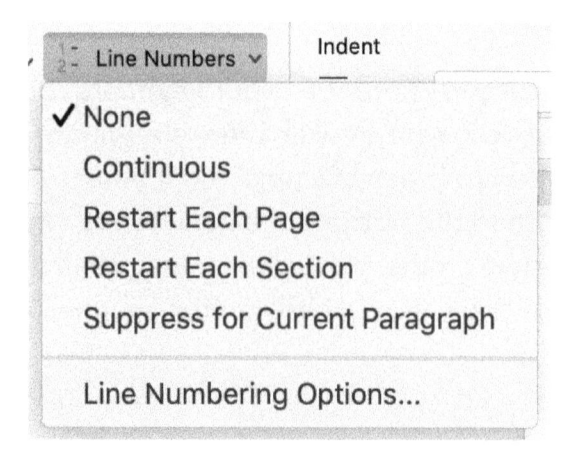

Hyphenation is telling Word that if you reach the end of the page, you want to hyphenate a word, so part of it appears on one line, and the other appears on the line below. It helps the justification look more even. By default it's turned on. If you want to add it, then you would use this option.

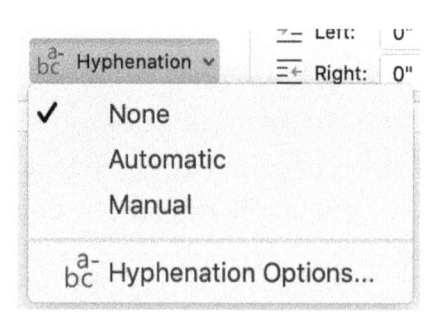

The next set of options tell Word how far over you want to indent and if you want spacing before and after paragraphs. By default it's at zero.

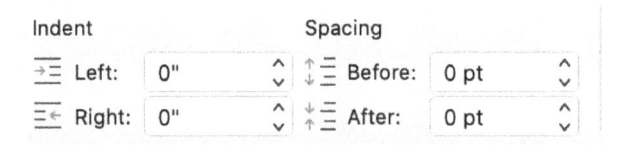

The last options help you edit where objects (like photos) are on the page. You'll probably notice that it's greyed out. That's because nothing is selected. When you select an image, it should light up.

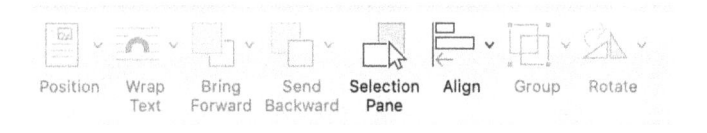

The first option, Position, lets you tell Word where you want the image to go with regard to text.

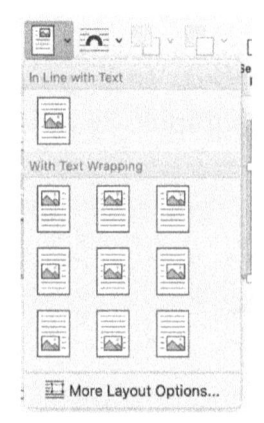

Similarly, the next option lets you tell Word how to wrap the text around an image.

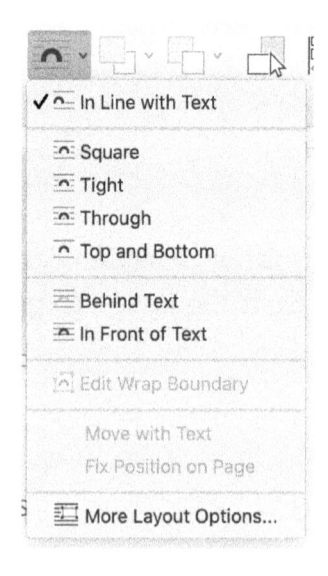

The next few options are a bit more complex—if you are working with a photo that has multiple layers, then this option would let you move the photos behind or in front of each other.

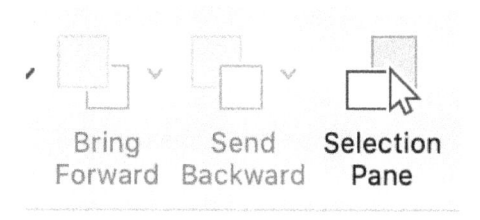

Bring Forward   Send Backward   Selection Pane

The next option lets you align the image.

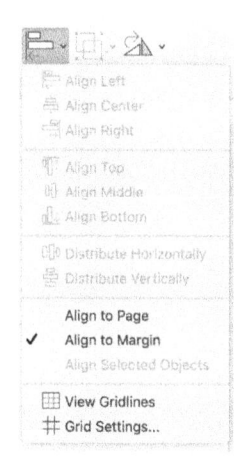

- Align Left
- Align Center
- Align Right
- Align Top
- Align Middle
- Align Bottom
- Distribute Horizontally
- Distribute Vertically
- Align to Page
- ✓ Align to Margin
- Align Selected Objects
- View Gridlines
- Grid Settings...

If there are several photos, you can group them all together and make them become one with the Group button; you can also click this button to ungroup images that are already grouped.

Group

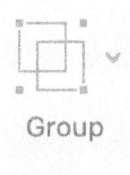

Finally, the last option lets you rotate an image either vertically or horizontally.

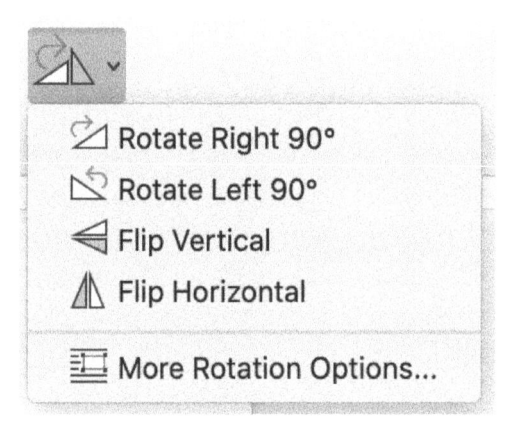

- Rotate Right 90°
- Rotate Left 90°
- Flip Vertical
- Flip Horizontal
- More Rotation Options...

[7]
THE REFERENCE RIBBON

If you are planning on using Word for research papers, then the Reference ribbon will be your best friend. It's also helpful for things like books if you have a novel you are burning to tell.

Starting from the left is the Table of Contents

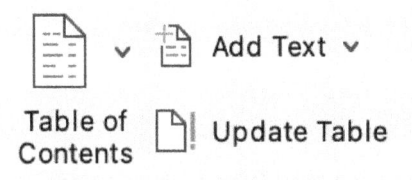

The table of contents drop-down lets you pick a style for your table of contents—that's the thing that goes in front of a book (i.e. Chapter 1 is page X). Once you pick your style, then it will add your table of contents wherever your cursor is.

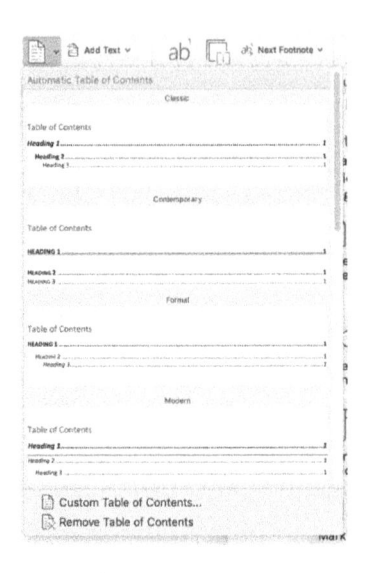

The table of contents is based off of Headings; so if you haven't used Heading 1, Heading 2, etc., then the table of contents will show up blank.

As you work through your book, you may find that your headings have changed—either you've added headings or the page numbering has changed. So you need to update the table of contents. You can do that by right clicking, then selecting Update Field.

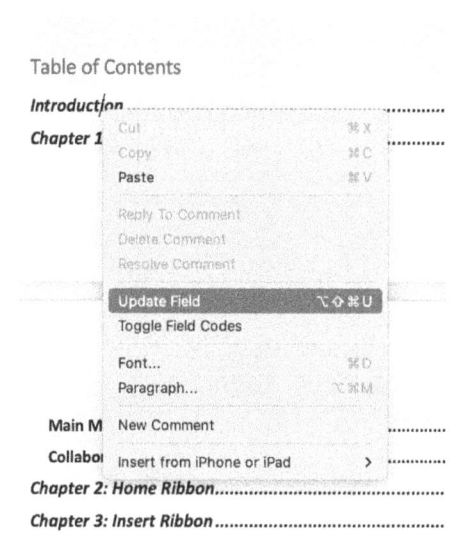

```
Table of Contents
Introduction ..........................................................
Chapter 1      Cut                         ⌘X    ..........
               Copy                        ⌘C
               Paste                       ⌘V

               Reply To Comment
               Delete Comment
               Resolve Comment

               Update Field              ⌥⇧⌘U
               Toggle Field Codes

               Font...                     ⌘D
               Paragraph...              ⌥⌘M

      Main M   New Comment                       ..........
      Collabo  Insert from iPhone or iPad  >     ..........
Chapter 2: Home Ribbon ........................................
Chapter 3: Insert Ribbon ......................................
```

If you don't want to add Headings, then you can also use the Add Text drop-down to add different levels.

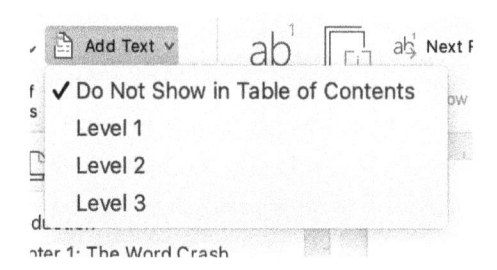

```
   Add Text ∨           ab¹         ab  Next
   ✓ Do Not Show in Table of Contents
     Level 1
     Level 2
     Level 3
```

Below that, you can click the Update Table anytime you don't want to right click and manually update it.

The next set of options is for Notes—there are two: footnotes and end notes. Anytime you want to add one, just go to the last letter of the word you want to add it to, and click the bottom.

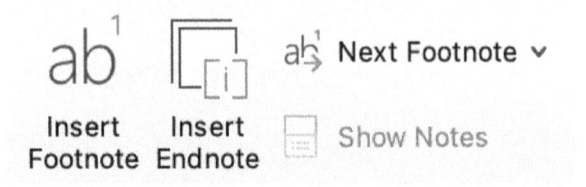

Insert Footnote   Insert Endnote   Show Notes   Next Footnote

What's the difference between endnotes and footnotes? Footnotes go at the bottom of the page the word appears; endnotes go at the end of the document.

Next is the research tools. These two tools (Smart Lookup and Researcher) are meant to keep you within Word so you don't have to go on the web to find what you need. But don't let the tool fool you: it is going on the Web to find it—it's just doing it within the software so you don't have to have your browser side by side.

Smart Lookup   Researcher

Smart Lookup is helpful if you need to look up info about a specific word—maybe you just need the definition, or maybe it's a scientific term and you need a little more; either way, highlight the word and click Smart Lookup. This will bring up a side panel with detailed information.

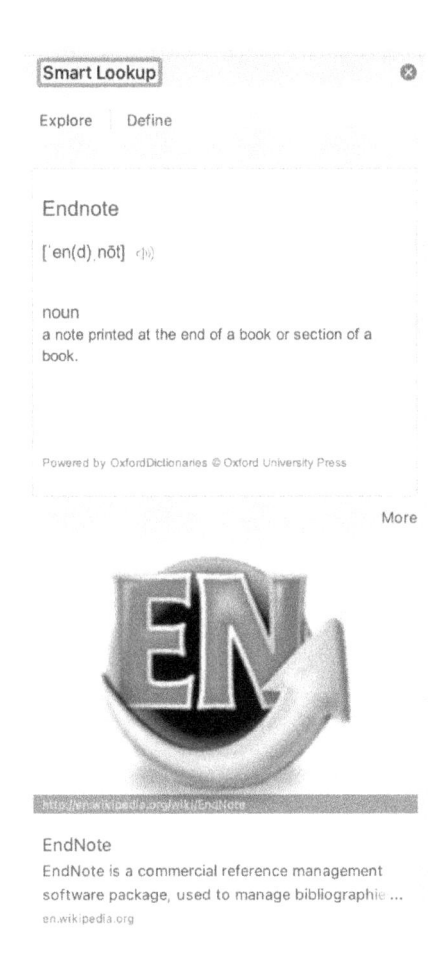

Researcher is when you don't want to look up a word that may or may not be in your document—you want to research a particular topic. It will ask you what you are looking for and also give you a handful of suggestions.

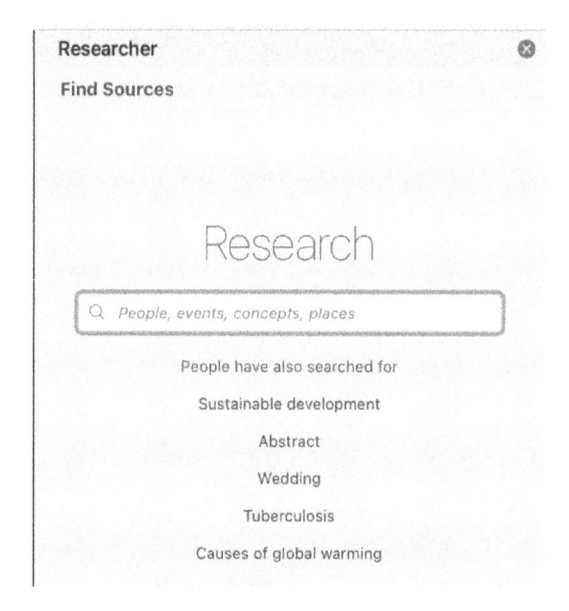

```
Researcher                                    ⊗
Find Sources



                        Research
          ⌕  People, events, concepts, places

                People have also searched for
                   Sustainable development
                          Abstract
                          Wedding
                        Tuberculosis
                   Causes of global warming
```

Once it returns the results, it will bring back some possible Web articles to explore.

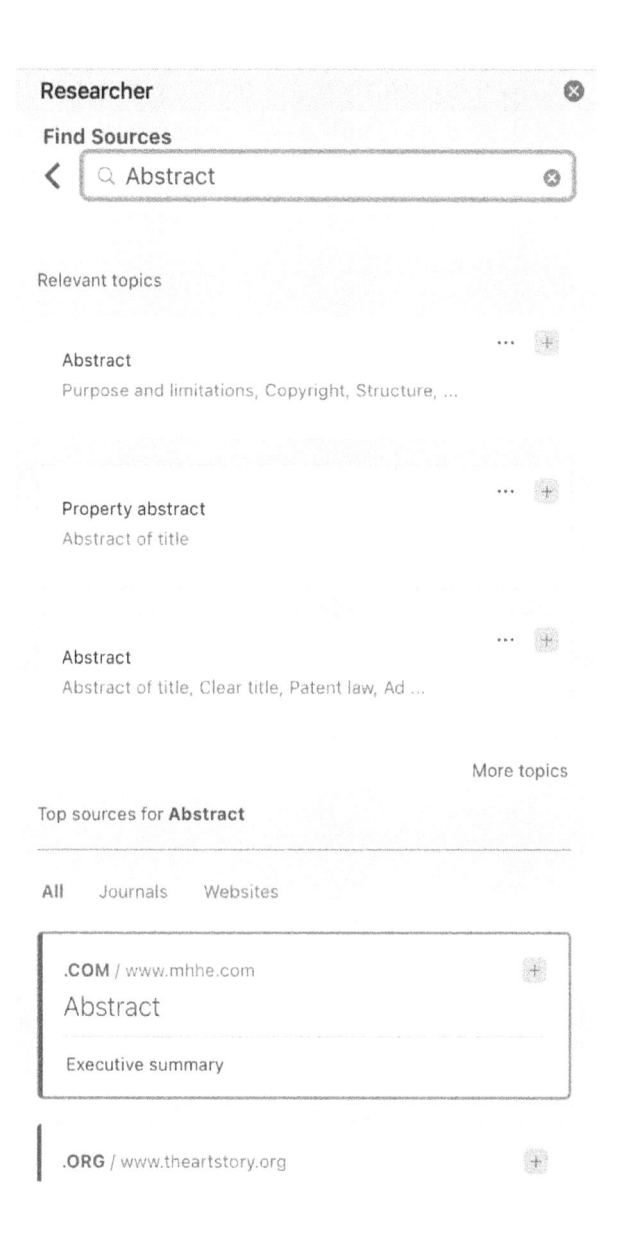

Researcher   ✕

Find Sources

❮ 🔍 Abstract ✕

Relevant topics

Abstract   ⋯ ＋
Purpose and limitations, Copyright, Structure, ...

Property abstract   ⋯ ＋
Abstract of title

Abstract   ⋯ ＋
Abstract of title, Clear title, Patent law, Ad ...

More topics

Top sources for **Abstract**

All   Journals   Websites

.COM / www.mhhe.com   ＋
Abstract

Executive summary

.ORG / www.theartstory.org   ＋

You'll notice that the articles don't look like the Web, but they are the same content you would find there. For example, the below example is all the content from the Wikipedia page of the topic, but it's formatted differently.

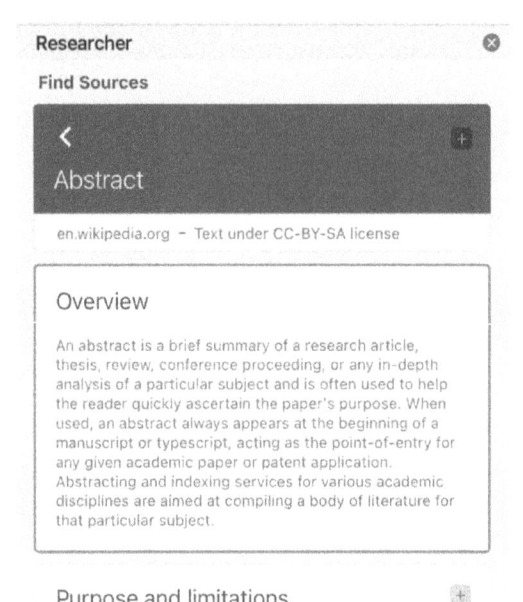

> **Researcher**
>
> **Find Sources**
>
> **‹ Abstract +**
>
> en.wikipedia.org – Text under CC-BY-SA license
>
> ### Overview
>
> An abstract is a brief summary of a research article, thesis, review, conference proceeding, or any in-depth analysis of a particular subject and is often used to help the reader quickly ascertain the paper's purpose. When used, an abstract always appears at the beginning of a manuscript or typescript, acting as the point-of-entry for any given academic paper or patent application. Abstracting and indexing services for various academic disciplines are aimed at compiling a body of literature for that particular subject.
>
> ### Purpose and limitations
>
> Academic literature uses the abstract to succinctly communicate complex research. An abstract may act as a stand-alone entity instead of a full paper. As such, an abstract is used by many organizations as the basis for selecting research that is proposed for presentation in the form of a poster, platform/oral presentation or workshop presentation at an academic conference. Most literature database search engines index only abstracts rather than providing the entire text of the paper. Full texts of scientific papers must often be purchased because of copyright and/or publisher fees and therefore the abstract is a significant selling point for the reprint or electronic form of the full text.
>
> The abstract can convey the main results and conclusions of a scientific article but the full text article must be

If you see something in the article that you want to include in your document, then highlight it and click Add and Cite; clicking Add will copy and paste it into the document, but it will not cite it. This is helpful if you are just creating a note to review later, but you want to be careful not to use it without a citation if you are turning it in for review.

Overview

An abstract is a brief summary of a research article, thesis, review, conference proceeding, or any in-depth analysis of a particular subject and is often used to help the reader quickly ascertain the paper's purpose. When used, an abstract always appears at the beginning of a manuscript or typescript, acting as the point-of-entry for any given academic paper or patent application. Abstracting and indexing services for various academic disciplines are aimed at compiling a body of literature for that particular subject.

Add and Cite
Add

Speaking of citations, that's what the next section is for.

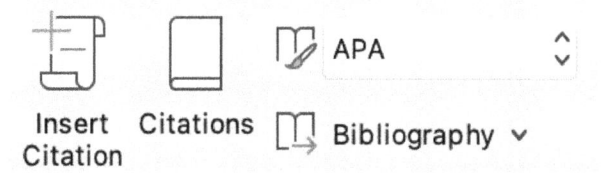

Insert Citation | Citations | APA | Bibliography

Before you add a citation, go to where it says APA and decide what method of citation you are using (i.e. Chicago style, MLA, etc.). The reason is when you click the Insert Citation, what's asked will be different because they're based on different guidelines.

When you click Insert Citation, it will bring up a menu that lets you add the information based on what type of material it is. In the example below, it says "Book" under source, but you can change that source to book section, article in a journal, article in a periodical, conference proceedings, report, web site, document from web site, electronic source, art, sound recording, performance, film, interview, patent, case, or miscellaneous.

Once you add the citation, you can click the Citations button to see a list of all the ones in the document. When you are ready, you can add a bibliography or work cited page. Just go to where in the document you want to add it, then click the Bibliography drop-down and pick the style.

Next is the captions and figures options.

The insert caption button adds or changes the text to a caption and lets you label it correctly. It's good for things like images and charts—to explain what a photo shows.

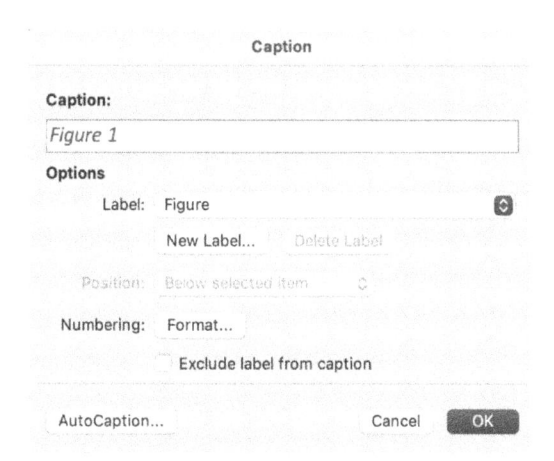

Figures lets you add labels to identify images. So if you said "In figure 1, it shows Y" then you can link to it correctly.

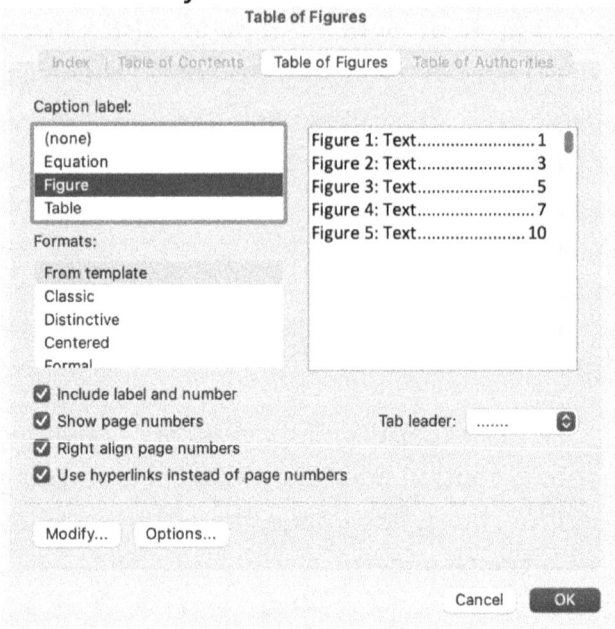

The final option is cross-reference. This option helps you link to related content within the document.

Scott La Counte | 79

> **Cross-reference**
>
> Reference type:
> [Numbered item]
>
> Insert reference to:
> [Paragraph number]
>
> ☑ Insert as hyperlink
> ☐ Include above/below
> ☐ Separate numbers with
>
> For which numbered item:
> 1. It formats your text quickly; so you don't have to apply a c...
> 2. It helps when you create your table of contents (if you are...
>
> [Cancel] [**Insert**]

If you plan to add an index, then you need to go through and mark all the words you want in the index using the Mark Entry button. Just hover over the word and click Mark Entry and add it.

Mark Entry   Insert Index
             Update Index

If you want to automate this a little, then you can click Insert Index, then select AutoMark; this will ask you to add a document that lists all the words you want in the Index. The easiest way to do this is to create a blank document, then add a table to that document, and then add a single column, and in each row add one word that you want in the index.

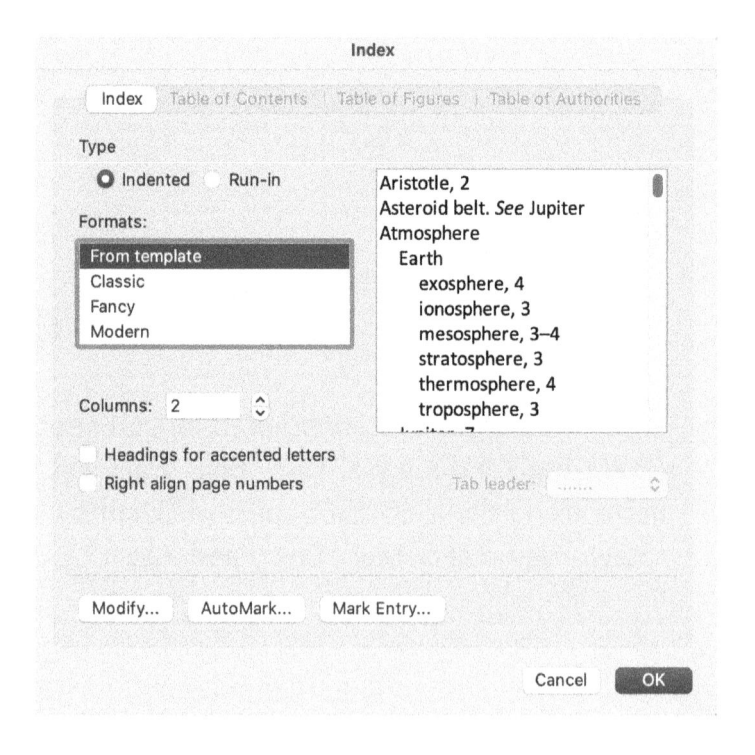

Finally, the last set of options is for the most advanced document types; it lets you mark citations and add a table of authorities—something that's mostly only used in legal documents.

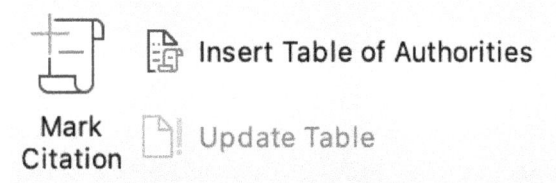

- Mark Citation
- Insert Table of Authorities
- Update Table

[8]
Mailings Ribbon

And now the moment I'm sure you've waited for: how do you simplify mailing out your annual Christmas letter?! First: don't! Everyone knows your family is perfect—do you really have to remind them? You do? Ok, then let's figure out how this ribbon works.

I'll preface what comes next by saying this will be simplified; the goal of this book is to get you set up as quickly as possible and Mailings can get a little…complicated. We aren't going to go into how to set up rules and filters. I'm going to keep it simple.

First things first, you got to set up what you are doing: an envelope or label that will go on the envelope. Most people will probably want labels just because it's far easier to do a single sheet than add envelopes to your printer and have each one run through individually.

Envelopes Labels

Next, you have to either merge a current list, or add recipients. Keeping with the theme of "simple" let's stick with the latter: Select Recipients.

Start Mail Merge   Select Recipients   Edit Recipient List   Filter Recipients

When you click this drop-down, you can use an existing list or even export it from your device or software. Let's stick with creating it from scratch by click on Create a New List.

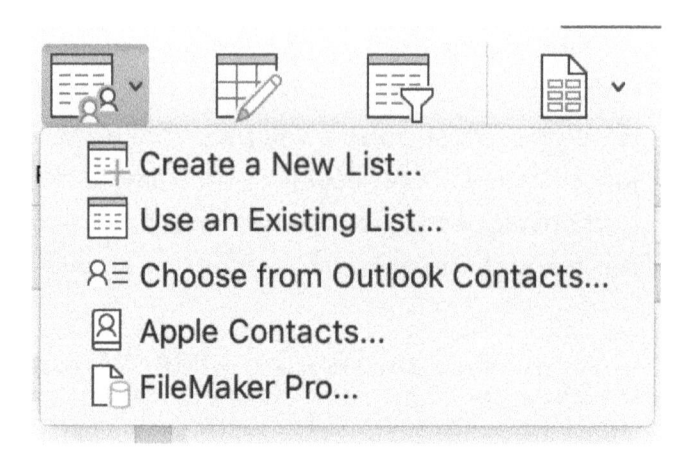

```
Create a New List...
Use an Existing List...
Choose from Outlook Contacts...
Apple Contacts...
FileMaker Pro...
```

Next you need to decide what information you are going to add about the person. You probably won't need to add things like phone number or company, so you can delete these by clicking on the minus button. Or you can use the + button to add an option. When you are satisfied, click Create.

This brings up a box to add in details about each person. Click the Add button to add the next option.

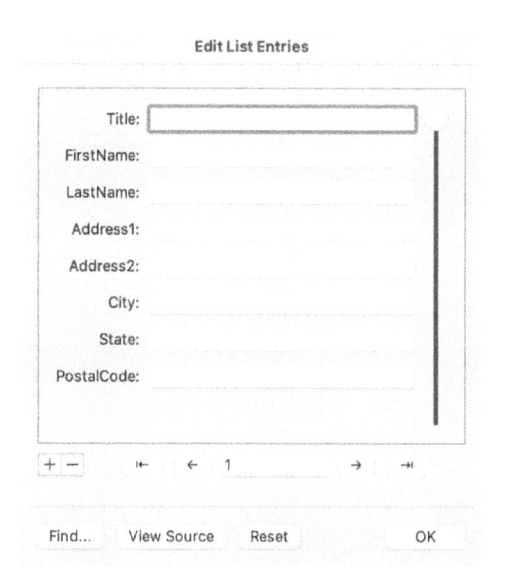

If all this is getting confusing and you want something that's easy, but takes more time, then just create a label document and add each one in manually.

[9]
REVIEW RIBBON

This is all great, but how do you spell check your document to make sure it makes sense to your reader? That and more is in the Review ribbon, so let's dig in.

The first option here is your beloved spell checker.

abc ✓
Spelling & Grammar

Clicking on this will bring up a new box that will immediately start going through your document. As you go through it, you can either click Change to make the change they selected, Change All to change any instance of the error, or use AutoCorrect to automatically do everything. You can also use the Add to add words it may not recognize, but are spelled correctly.

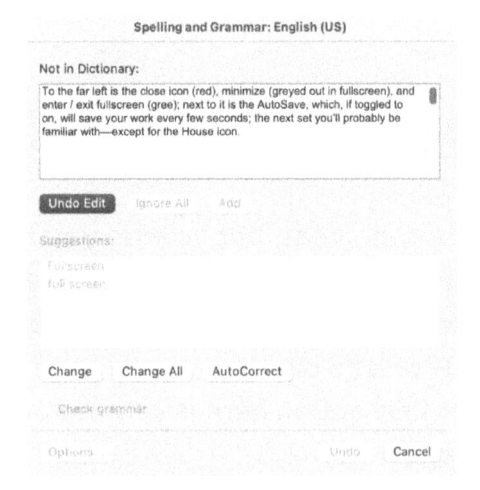

Spelling and Grammar: English (US)

Not in Dictionary:

To the far left is the close icon (red), minimize (greyed out in fullscreen), and enter / exit fullscreen (gree); next to it is the AutoSave, which, if toggled to on, will save your work every few seconds; the next set you'll probably be familiar with—except for the House icon.

Undo Edit   Ignore All   Add

Suggestions:
Fullscreen
full screen

Change   Change All   AutoCorrect

Check grammar

Options   Undo   Cancel

The other two options in this section are Thesaurus (highlight a word and click this to bring up a thesaurus for the word) and the word counter.

If you are like me—and lots of other people—you may have this nasty habit of reading your writing the way it should be...not the way it is. Next to the spell checker is a very useful readback tool called Read Aloud.

Read Aloud

When you click it (or highlight text to select only a section) it will begin reading back what is on the page to help you catch errors you might miss by reading it yourself. You can use the double arrows to skip words (or go back) and the config button to change the reader speed or narrator.

The Check Accessibility option will probably not be used by most people; this helps you find ways to improve the document for people with an impairment—providing alternative text for pictures, for example, so if a person can't see, they can have the photo explained.

Check Accessibility

Like many other options in this section, the next two options probably will not be used by the average user; they are language tools. The first option, Translate, will turn either a portion of the text (or the entire document) into one of dozens of different languages. Results vary, so this is not something you want to do in a professional document—it will sound very strange to someone who speaks the language natively.

Translate Language

The next button, Language, lets you tell Word what Language the text is. So if you are spell checking a document it doesn't get to a small chunk that is in, Spanish for example, and say the text is incorrect—it will recognized that it is a different language and move on.

You can quickly get to comments from the Comments option just above any ribbon, but you can also access it on the Review ribbon.

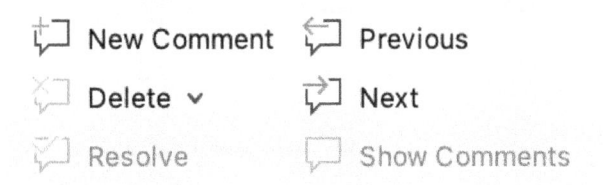

New Comment   Previous
Delete   Next
Resolve   Show Comments

If you are collaborating on a document, toggling Track Changes to on will show any changes made in a document—so you know who did what.

OFF   All Markup
Track Changes   Markup Options

Reviewing lets you see a summary of what was changed.

Reviewing

When you get a document returned to you that has changes, you can use the Accept / Reject buttons to go through the document and either remove or add a change.

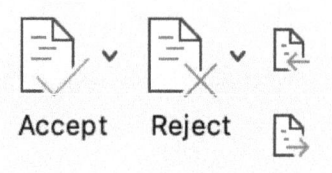

Accept   Reject

Compare lets you see different versions of a document.

Compare

Protect lets you add password protection to your document.

Protect

[10]
View Ribbon

The last non-hidden menu in the ribbon is View. I say non-hidden because, as I'll show in the forthcoming chapters, there are formatting menus that appear when things are selected.

As the name implies, view lets you view things—who knew, right? The options are all pretty straightforward, but it still helps to know they exist and what their functionality is.

The first four options change the way things look in terms of the actual page; the other ones just give enhancement. The four options are print layout, web layout, outline, and draft.

Print Layout   Web Layout   Outline   Draft

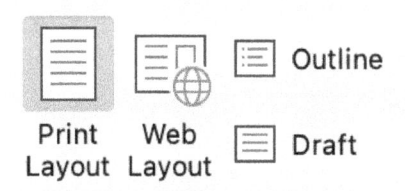

Print layout will be the only layout most users will use; web layout is one long scrolling document with no page breaks, outline lets you see formatting (such as if there's a hard return), and draft is a very minimal view of your document without things like style and images.

Focus and Immersive Reader are the next two options, and they each take away distractions (like menu options) so it's easier to read.

Focus   Immersive Reader

The next options show or hide different menus—if you don't want to see the ruler bar, for example. Gridlines will add a grid to your document (it won't show up when you print). Navigation Pane will show the navigational structure of your document (if you have added headings).

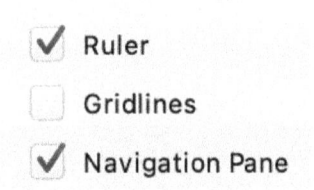

☑ Ruler
☐ Gridlines
☑ Navigation Pane

If you need to zoom in or out, you can use the next set of options. You can also use the Multiple Pages option to show two pages side-by-side.

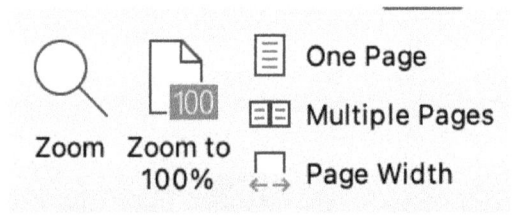

Zoom   Zoom to 100%   One Page   Multiple Pages   Page Width

If you want to multitask with two different documents, you can use the next three options.

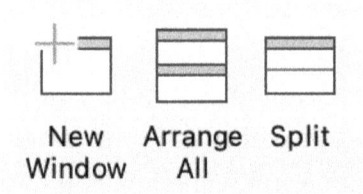

New Window   Arrange All   Split

The last option is for Macros. This is an advanced tool that you will not need for basic editing.

Macros

[11]

FORMATTING PHOTOS AND SHAPES

The Formatting menu is somewhat of a hidden menu. What does that mean? It means you won't see it in your ribbon until you click a photo. Click a photo and suddenly it appears in your ribbon.

The first option you see is Remove Background, which will do it's best to remove the background of a photo.

Remove Background

What do I mean by "best"? Let's look. Below is a normal photo that has a background.

When I do remove background, the results come out like the below. You can adjust it to not remove certain areas, but this feature really works best when you have a solid background.

The next set of options are for making enhancements to the photo—making the colors brighter, softer, or more transparent, for example.

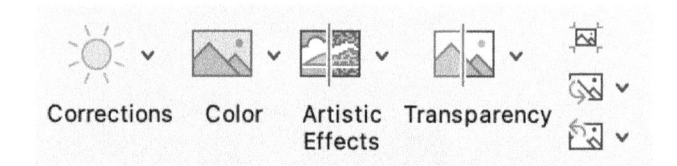

Corrections will try and enhance the brightness; Color will give it a color hue; Transparency will give it a lightened look, so it can appear in the background—as a watermark, for example. Finally, those three options on the far-right side? The top is to compress your image—so if your document is huge because you have lots of photos and you want it smaller, you could use this to compress the images into something with less resolution—it's nice for emailing, but not as nice for printing. The middle option is used to change the photo—replacing it with an alternative photo; and the bottom photo is used to reset any changes you have made.

The next set of options help your image stand out with different borders. You can give it a 3D border, for example, or change it to an oval shape.

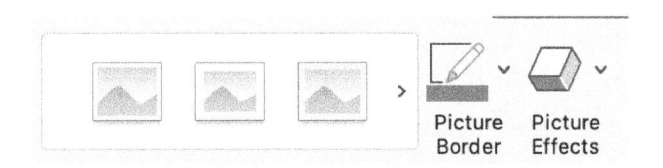

Picture Border   Picture Effects

Alt Text is an accessibility feature; this lets you add text for someone who is visually impaired and having the text read to them vs. reading it themselves; it would narrate what the photo is.

Alt Text

The alignment section is next; this helps you with placement of the photo. The one that is used the most is the Wrap Text option; this option determines if the text will wrap around the image or if it will have text on top and bottom of it (or even text going through it).

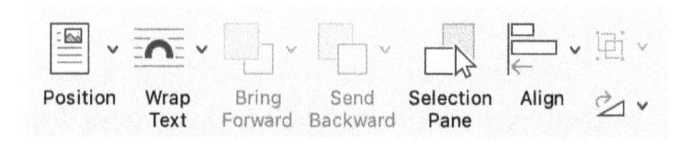

Position Wrap Bring Send Selection Align
          Text Forward Backward Pane

The cropping tools is the next section; you can use crop to reduce the image and crop out certain areas—if it's a picture of a whole person, for example, but you only want to show the face.

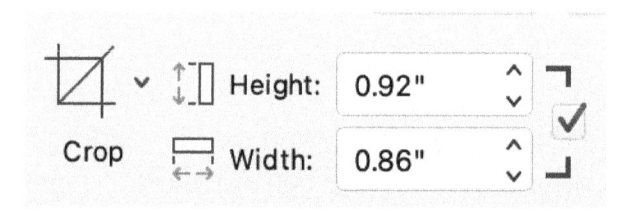

Crop Height: 0.92"
      Width: 0.86"

Finally, the Format Pane option can add glows and edges to a photo to make it pop a little more.

Format Pane

[12]
Let's Get Creative!

Now that you know where things are and what they do, let's wrap up by doing an actual document so you can see hands on how it all comes together. In this chapter we are going to create a Christmas newsletter your grandma will be proud of. Are you already a grandma? Well your children are about to be dazzled!

There's two ways you can do this: the easy way and the not so easy way. I'll show you quickly the easy way, but in this exercise, we will do it the longer, more custom way (i.e. the harder way). I'm doing that because I want to make sure you know how all the features work.

The easy way will have you go up to your menu bar and select File > New from Template.

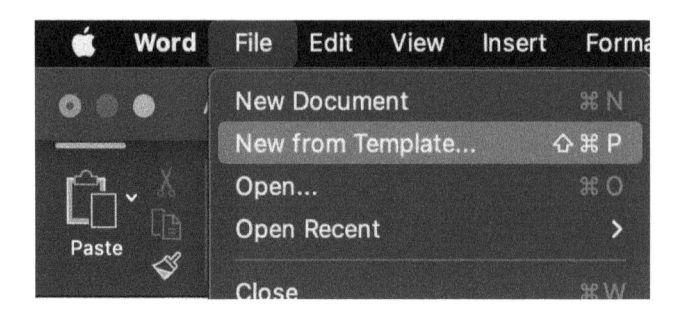

This will bring up all the possible templates in Word (hint: there's a lot of them); the easiest way to find the right template is to search for it. You can search for resumes, fliers, cover letters, etc. But in this example, just type in "Newsletter."

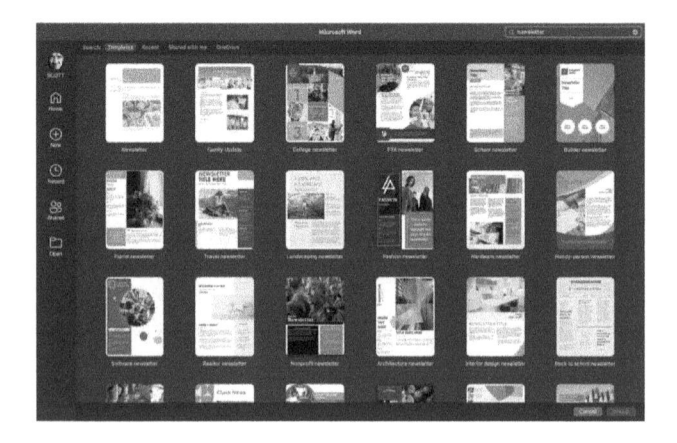

See all the newsletters that pop up?! There's something for everyone. When you find the one you want, just click on it, and click the Create button in the lower right corner. Now all you have to do is replace the text and images in it.

Simple, right? Now let's make it difficult!

Let's start by adding some fun WordArt at the top of the page. That's going to be in the Insert ribbon menu near the far-right side.

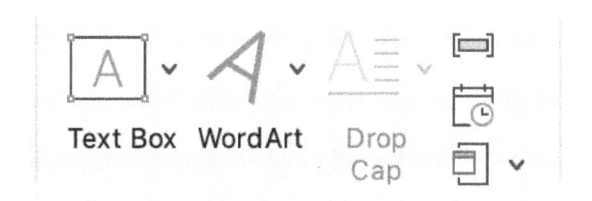

This will bring up a drop-down box that lets you pick the right kind of shading you want; pick whatever you want (and remember, anytime you make a mistake, just do Edit > Undo or CTRL+Z to undo the changes).

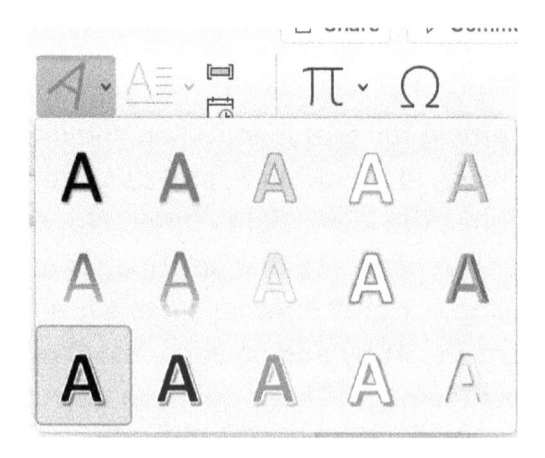

Now add in your text.

Christmas Newsletter

It's starting to look good, but it's also aligned wrong. You don't want a fancy title like that hanging out in the top middle of the page. You want it in the middle. You can click and drag it, or you could be more precise by going to the Smart Format ribbon (hint: it only shows up when you click the image), then click Arrange > Position > Position in Top Center.

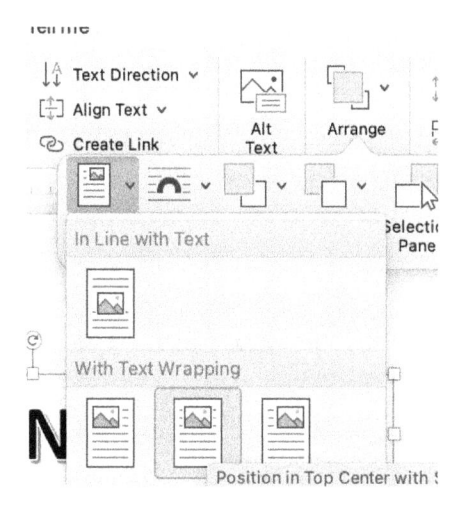

Nice! But the text is currently black. That isn't very festive! Highlight the text, then go to the Home menu and click the text color option. I'm going to pick a more Christmas-y red.

While we are on the menu, let's make the size larger. Notice in the example below, I just added the custom size, "50"? You don't have to use the predefined sizes—you can even use halves (i.e. 55.5).

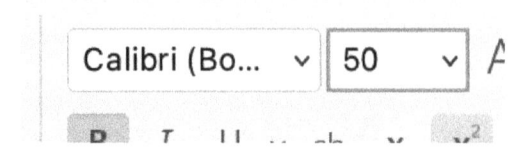

Now let's add a line under the word. You could technically do this by going to Insert > Shape > Line; but the quicker way to do it is to type three "---" and then hit enter.

See how the dashes immediately become one solid line? Cool, right?!

Christmas Newsletter

The next thing all great newsletters do is brag about how amazing their year has been. Unfortunately, my the most amazing thing that happened to me this year is I ordered a six piece Chicken McNugget and they gave me seven pieces instead. So for this example, I'm just going to copy the same sentence several times. The idea is just to create text that we will format.

Christmas Newsletter

THIS IS SOME TEXT ABOUT HOW AWESOME MY YEAR HAS BEEN! THIS IS SOME

Once you have enough text to format, highlight it, then go to the layout ribbon, and select the Columns icon and pick the desired number of columns. I'll pick three.

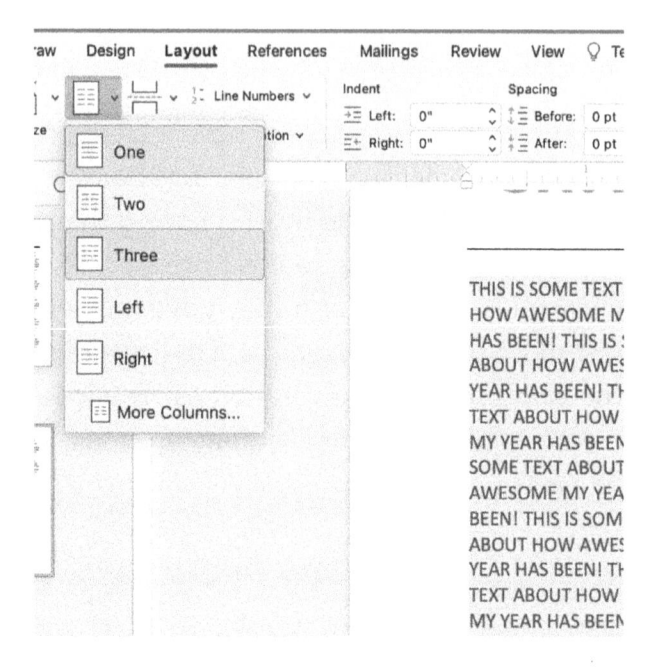

You should now have several evenly split columns. It looks good, but there's one small problem—the gap between each column seems a bit big. Let's fix that.

Christmas Newsletter

THIS IS SOME TEXT ABOUT HOW AWESOME MY YEAR HAS BEEN! THIS IS SOME TEXT ABOUT HOW AWESOME MY YEAR HAS BEEN! THIS IS SOME TEXT ABOUT HOW AWESOME MY YEAR HAS BEEN! THIS IS SOME TEXT ABOUT HOW AWESOME MY YEAR HAS BEEN! THIS IS SOME TEXT ABOUT HOW AWESOME MY YEAR HAS BEEN! THIS IS SOME TEXT ABOUT HOW AWESOME

BEEN! THIS IS SOME TEXT ABOUT HOW AWESOME MY YEAR HAS BEEN! THIS IS SOME TEXT ABOUT HOW AWESOME MY YEAR HAS BEEN! THIS IS SOME TEXT ABOUT HOW AWESOME MY YEAR HAS BEEN! THIS IS SOME TEXT ABOUT HOW AWESOME MY YEAR HAS BEEN! THIS IS SOME TEXT ABOUT HOW AWESOME MY YEAR HAS BEEN! THIS IS SOME TEXT ABOUT HOW

HAS BEEN! THIS IS SOME TEXT ABOUT HOW AWESOME MY YEAR HAS BEEN! THIS IS SOME TEXT ABOUT HOW AWESOME MY YEAR HAS BEEN! THIS IS SOME TEXT ABOUT HOW AWESOME MY YEAR HAS BEEN! THIS IS SOME TEXT ABOUT HOW AWESOME MY YEAR HAS BEEN! THIS IS SOME TEXT ABOUT HOW AWESOME MY YEAR HAS BEEN! THIS IS SOME TEXT ABOUT

The first thing I'm going to do is adjust the margin of the entire doc. Normally you want a one inch margin; since this is a newsletter, we can go with smaller. Let's make it 0.3. Go to the Layout ribbon menu, then click the Margins icon, and pick Custom Margins on the bottom.

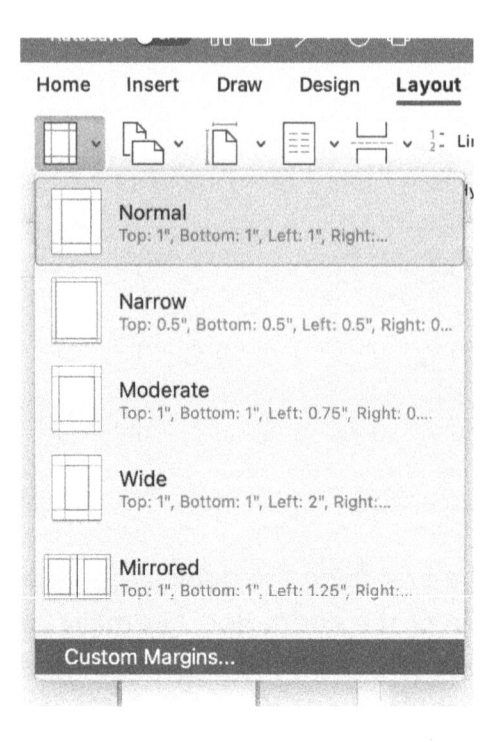

From here, add in 0.3" for your Top, Bottom, Left, Right; leave the gutter as zero, then click OK. Keep in mind that some printers won't print with thin margins, so you might have to make the margins bigger.

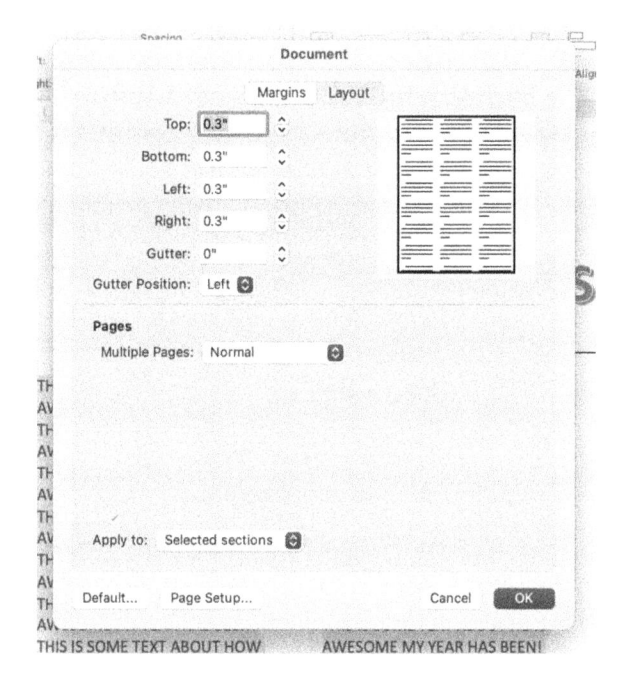

Once you click OK, you'll immediately see the margins are now smaller and there's more text fitting on the screen.

This is great, but what about that white space between the columns? Go to Format > Columns.

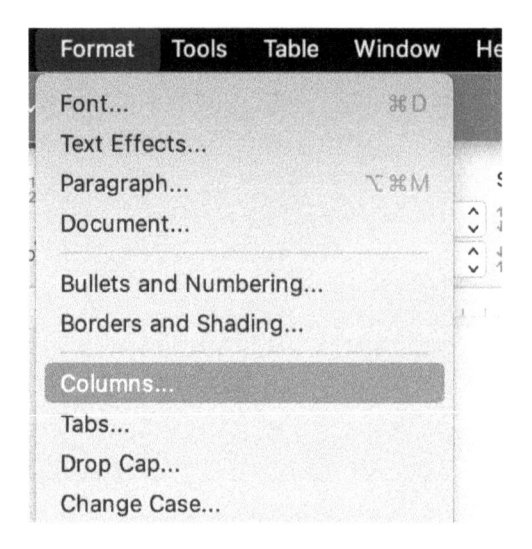

```
Format    Tools    Table    Window    He
 Font...                        ⌘D
 Text Effects...
 Paragraph...                   ⌥⌘M
 Document...

 Bullets and Numbering...
 Borders and Shading...

 Columns...
 Tabs...
 Drop Cap...
 Change Case...
```

This brings up the format menu; if you want to, you can use this menu to change the amount of columns and even make some columns thinner than others. For our dazzling Christmas newsletter, we want to keep it simple and just reduce the spacing in between the columns. So in that spacing area, change 0.5" to 0.2".

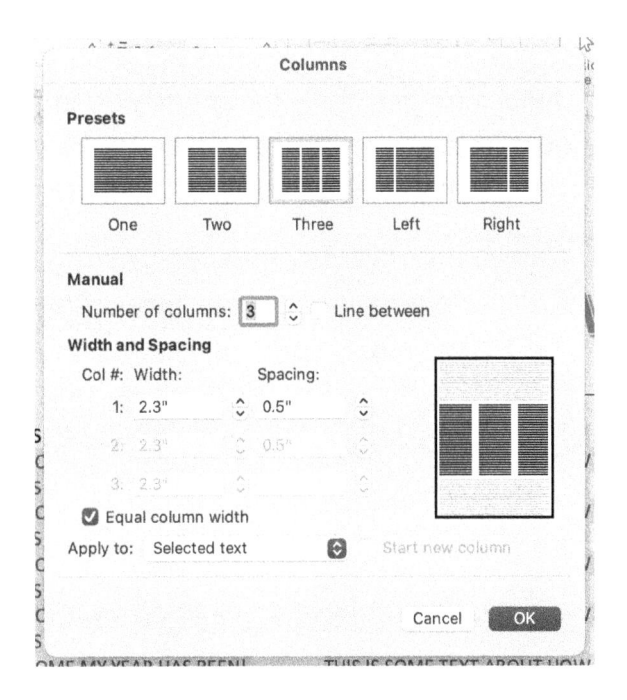

It doesn't sound like a lot, but the difference is actually pretty noticeable.

Now let's get really fancy and add in amazing photos from our year. Go to Insert > Pictures > Picture from File and find some photos on your computer.

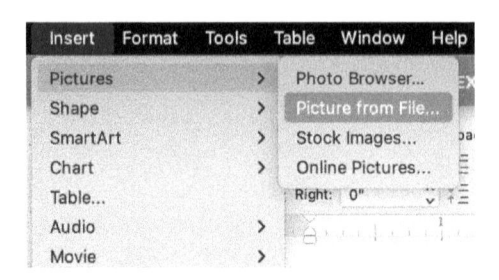

Again, I didn't have an exciting year and don't even have a photo of those seven Chicken McNuggets! So, I'll just add in an old book cover. Use anything you like. Notice how it's right smack in the middle of the text? Not exactly newsletter-y is it? Let's fix that!

Click the image, then go to Picture Format and click the Wrap Text icon; then select Square (instead of In Line with Text).

Nothing happens, right? Wrong! It happened, you just can't see it yet. While clicking on the image, drag it to the left or right; see how the text is wrapping around it? You can now have it in between columns, which is more what you'd expect in a newsletter.

But it's still missing something other snazzy Christmas newsletters have with their photos: captions! How else will they know what's so impressive about the photo? To add one, right click on the image and click Insert Caption.

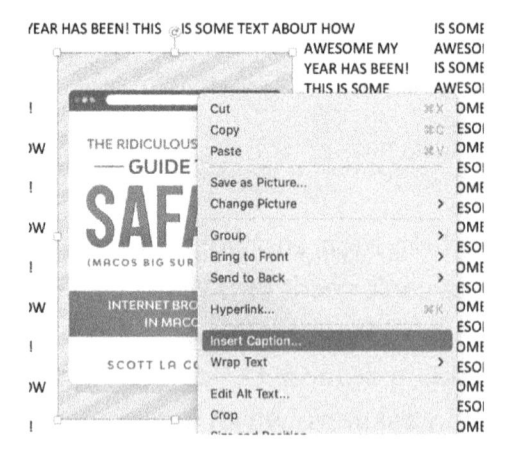

Type what you want the caption to say, then click OK.

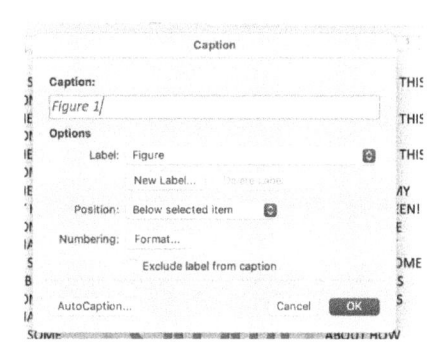

A caption now appears below the image.

It still isn't feeling very festive to me, so let's add a Christmas image in the background as a watermark. Click the Insert ribbon menu, then click the Icons button.

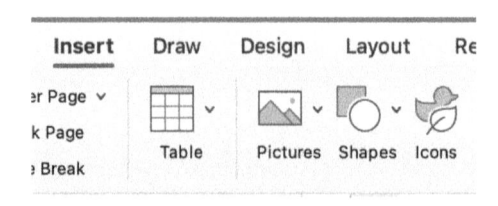

From here, search for "Christmas." I'll pick a tree.

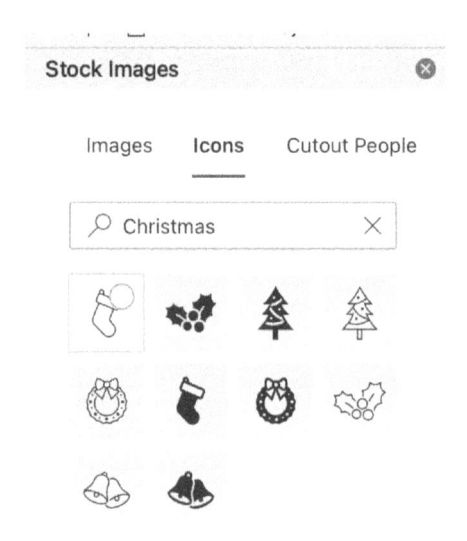

It's in the foreground now; but a watermark goes in the background, so how do we change that?

First let's follow the steps above to change the wrapping to Square; then make it larger—make it fill the entire page.

Next, right click the image and click Format Graphic.

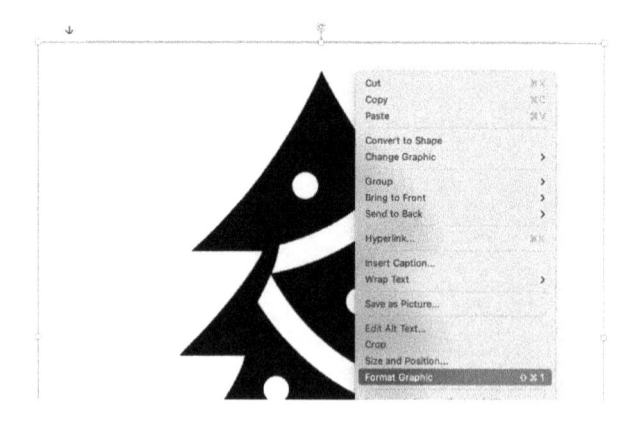

In the format pane, change the transparency to 75% (you can make it whatever you want).

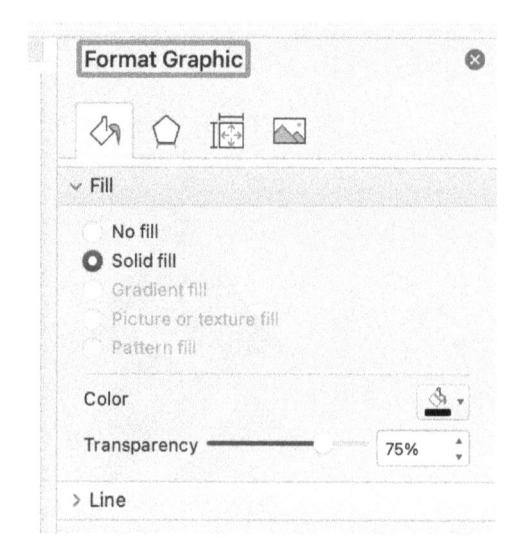

Now go to the Graphics Format ribbon (remember you have to click the image to see it) and change the wrap to Behind Text.

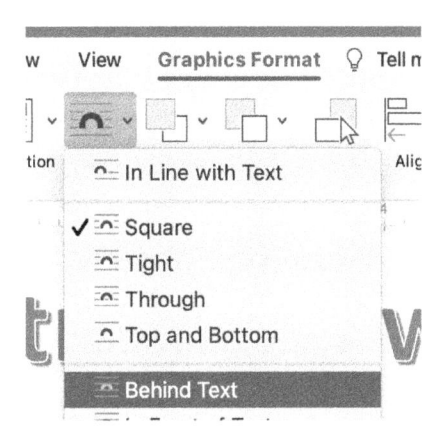

You now have a watermark nestled behind your text. If it's too bright, you can always go back and adjust the transparency.

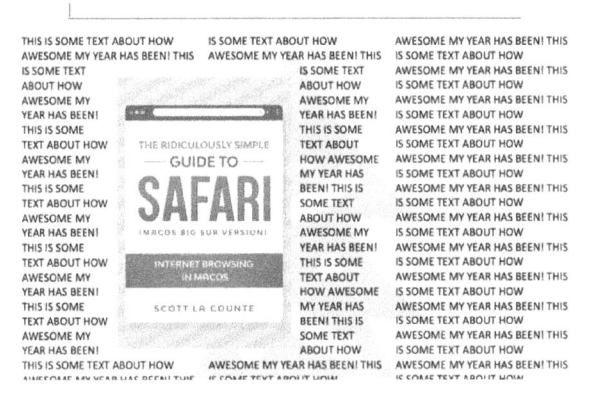

Now that you've seen how to create a newsletter, you can always return to using a template and add in some of these tricks we've just learned.

[13]
Accessibility

Word offers several accessibility features that help people who are visually or hearing impaired. Let's start with some that will help you if you have trouble typing.

Dictation and Read Aloud

Word must know that for every person out there that can type 200 words per minute (WPM) there's a person who types with two fingers at a speed of a little less than one word a minute—and if you are that person, then welcome to the club! Fortunate for you, the days of typing may be over for you. You can speak what you want to type.

To do speak to type, go to the Home Ribbon and click on the Dictate button.

Dictate

This is going to open a floating box that says "Listening...". You can click and hold it to drag it around the screen.

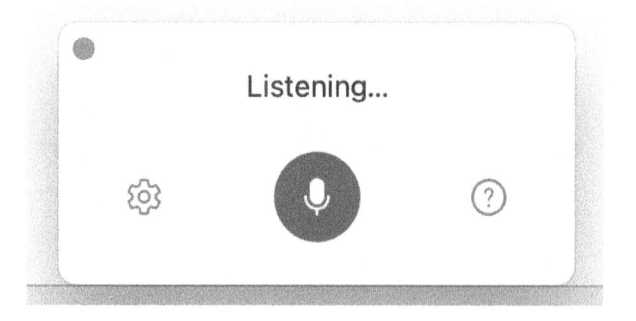

Listening...

Listening means that the microphone is turned on and anything you say will be shown in Word;

there's a slight delay, so give it a handful of seconds if it doesn't appear right away.

By default, the language is set to English (United States); what if you are speaking another language? Or what if you happen to be speaking English but with a UK accent? Click the little config button on the box, and select the language from the dropdown.

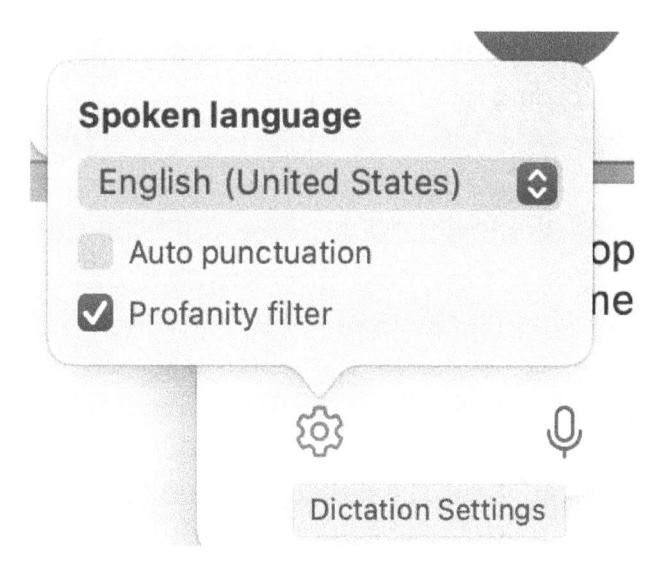

On the same config button as the drop down, you'll see two other options:
1. Auto punctuation
2. Profanity filter

Auto puntuation will listen and detect grammar; so if it detects what you have just spoke is a question, then it will add a question mark. If it detects you need a comma, it will add one for you. It's surprisingly good at this. Profanity filter is a censor of sorts—accidentally drop profanity in that company memo? It won't add it. In it's place it will add *******.

If you want to keep dictation open, but don't want it to listen for a few moments, then just click the microphone; it will turn blue to white—white means the microphone is off and it's no longer recording what you say.

Now that it's all typed up, what if you prefer to listen to it than read it? Easy! Click the Review ribbon, then click the Read Aloud button.

This opens up a small box that has a play, fast-forward, rewind, and config button.

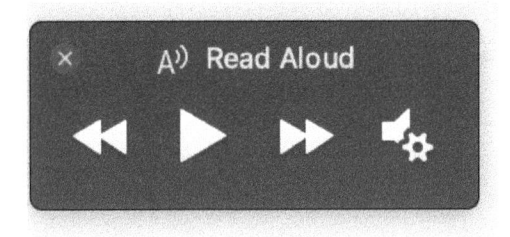

To read text, you must first highlight what you want read back, then click the play button; if you hit play without highlighting anything, then nothing will happen. Once it's reading then the fast-forward and rewind button will go back several seconds.

If you want the narrator to speak faster or slower, then click the config button and drag the slider to the right or left. You can also use the config button to select a different narrator—as of this writing, there are two male and two female voices.

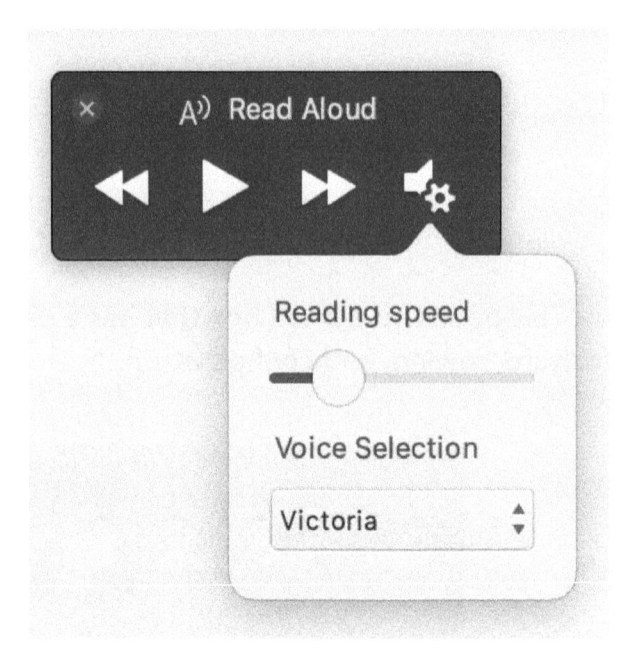

If you aren't happy with how Word's dictation feature works, then there's a lot of third-party solutions that you can use for dictation, and then import into word. One of the more popular ones is Dragon Speech.

Zooming

As covered earlier in this book, there are several viewing options in the View Ribbon. This includes zooming and immersive reading. But that requires you to click the ribbon and find the option. There's a quicker way.

On the bottom of the word document is a thin line with several more options. One of these options is a slider for zooming in and out. It will probably say 142%--that's the default. That means what you are looking at on the screen right now is actually larger than what would be printed out.

Index

A

Accessibility 90
Addons 35

B

Bibliography 77

C

Caption 118
Charts 33
Citation 76
Colors 50
Columns 59, 110, 114

D

Dictate 23

F

Figures 78
Formatting 98

H

Heading 21, 49, 68
Headings 68, 69
Hyphenation 62

L

Language 91

M

Macros 97
Mailings 82

P

Pictures 116
Print 95

R

Reference 67
Reviewing 91

S

Shapes 30, 98
Style 22
Symbols 45

T

Table 3, 27, 67, 69
Table of Contents 3, 67
Themes 49
Track Changes 13, 91
Translate 90

W

Watermark 53

Wrap Text 101, 117

ABOUT THE AUTHOR

Scott La Counte is a technologist, librarian and writer. His first book, *Quiet, Please: Dispatches from a Public Librarian* (Da Capo 2008) was the editor's choice for the Chicago Tribune and a Discovery title for the Los Angeles Times; in 2011, he published the YA book The N00b Warriors, which became a #1 Amazon bestseller; his most recent book is *#OrganicJesus: Finding Your Way to an Unprocessed, GMO-Free Christianity* (Kregel 2016).

He has written dozens of best-selling how-to guides on tech products.

You can connect with him at ScottDouglas.org.

Lightning Source UK Ltd.
Milton Keynes UK
UKHW010142170822
407391UK00006B/415